WILDLIFE ON FARMS

— How to conserve native animals —

David Lindenmayer, Andrew Claridge,
Donna Hazell, Damian Michael, Mason Crane,
Christopher MacGregor and Ross Cunningham

CSIRO
PUBLISHING

National Library of Australia Cataloguing-in-Publication entry:

   Wildlife on farms: how to conserve native animals.

   Includes index.

   ISBN 0 643 06866 X.

   1. Agricultural conservation – Australia. 2. Wildlife conservation – Australia. I. Lindenmayer, David.

   639.90994

Available from:
CSIRO PUBLISHING
150 Oxford Street (PO Box 1139)
Collingwood VIC 3066
Australia

Telephone: +61 3 9662 7666
Freecall: 1800 645 051 (Australia only)
Fax: +61 3 9662 7555
Email: publishing.sales@csiro.au
Web site: www.publish.csiro.au

Cover photos: Esther Beaton, David Lindenmayer, Andrew Claridge, Mike Greer (Chicago Zoological Society) and Ian R McCann/Nature Focus.
Set in Minion 10/12
Cover design and text design by James Kelly
Printed in Australia by Impact Printing

WILDLIFE

Seven Da~ an
ned on

University

Foreword

As the whole community will benefit in the long run from considered and informed environmental management, *Wildlife on Farms: How to conserve native animals* is important to us all. Commercial land mangers have long recognised the need for environmentally aware and sensitive practices to maintain the health of their areas; the Landcare movement in Australia has its origins in the shared concerns of farmers and environmentalists. However, as the book shows, translating these concerns into practical action is somewhat more challenging.

The reason for this is because even as environmental awareness develops and matures in the wider Australian community, implementing environmentally focused programs comes up against two main barriers. The first is the limited current knowledge we have on managing ecosystem interactions—these are complex, not constant, localised and they change over time. The other barrier is that many of the recent environmental programs impose limitations and costs on land managers that have a negative effect on commercial balance sheets. This book contributes to overcoming both obstacles as it provides practical information on wildlife conservation on-farm (or, in the current jargon, 'off-reserve conservation'), and it recognises that the voluntary practices proposed may well have productivity trade-offs.

Commercial land managers generally have positive attitudes towards the environment. *Wildlife on Farms* will provide useful support for them. It is also hoped that some of the more hesitant land managers will be encouraged to take steps in the directions proposed.

As the book notes, there are still many knowledge gaps including the critical area of the role of production lands in wildlife conservation. How can this aspect be tied in with conserved habitat in the conservation of wildlife? Farm management practices such as the cultivation of introduced perennial grasses, alternative 'litter' produced by commercial herbivores, the role of set stocking versus more intensive 'rotations', the increased availability of water, growing annual and perennial crops (including tree crops), all impact on wildlife habitat. There are also contentious socio-environmental issues which can easily overwhelm on-farm wildlife programs. For instance there are virtually uncontrolled and enormous populations of foxes, feral cats, pigs and now the increasing menace of feral dogs. Hesitant and conflicting community views at times can place concern for these animals' welfare ahead of concerns about the impacts these pests have on commercial animals and wildlife. Similarly, these attitudes also limit essential public pest control programs. For the sake of the environment our attitudes to managing challenges such as these pests need to change.

Through books such as *Wildlife on Farms* we look forward to a more informed and mature approach in Australia to managing our environment in a sustainable and productive way. Sustainability demands that the current largely negative impact of environmental programs on land managers is rectified so that the wider environmental gains to the community are shared by the landholders and that this is reflected in their balance sheets. Land managers cannot be expected to bear all the costs. Both practical and positive methods are needed for land managers—our front-line operational environmentalists—to keep their farms productive and to conserve wildlife as far as possible. This book provides a readable step in that direction, providing often simple changes to traditional ways that can have a marked positive effect on native wildlife.

As a practical land manager I hope that other land managers as well as regulators adopt this as an essential handbook. I also ask that they take the opportunity to provide feedback to the authors so our shared environmental knowledge and understanding continues to grow.

John Lowe
'Kerrabee', Bulga Creek, ACT

Preface

Many people want to know more about the native animals on their land and how they can conserve them. All animals need habitat—without it they will not survive. This book looks at the key habitats that occur on farms. These are trees, understorey trees and shrubs, fallen logs, rock piles, native grasses, creeks, wetlands and farm dams. The book shows how important these habitats are for many native mammals, birds, reptiles and frogs. We also outline ways of conserving habitats on farms—ways that may be incorporated into normal management practices so that farming businesses still run productively.

By focusing on the habitats of birds and other animals and how to manage them, we hope this book will contribute to the conservation of Australia's natural heritage so that we can share the experience of our extraordinary wildlife with future generations.

David Lindenmayer
Andrew Claridge
Donna Hazell
Damian Michael
Mason Crane
Christopher MacGregor
Ross Cunningham

Acknowledgements

This book was made possible through the generous support of Jim Atkinson and Di Stockbridge, Land and Water Australia and the Australian Research Council. Jann Williams and Phil Price from Land and Water Australia have been valuable supporters of our work for many years. John Lowe, Warren Mortlock, Henry Nix, Will Osborne, Dave Hunter, Nicki Taws, Jim Viggers, Karen Viggers, Jann Williams and Stephen Young made many useful comments on earlier versions of the manuscript. Monica Ruibal most capably assisted with many of the fiddly tasks associated with this book such as collecting literature and other material. McComas Taylor, Nick Alexander and Anne Findlay did a terrific job in editing what proved to be a very difficult text to write.

Nick Alexander from CSIRO Publishing championed this work through his keen support of the idea when it was first proposed. Esther Beaton, Auscape and Nature Focus assisted greatly in providing the photographic material for this book.

Many of the PhD students at the Centre for Resource and Environmental Studies provided much of the stimulus for this book, in particular Joern Fischer, Adrian Manning and Ioan Fazey. We are most grateful to the landowners of Tumut, Adjungbilly, Riverina and Braidwood regions of southern New South Wales who alerted us to the need for the sort of information that we have tried to present in this short book. Andrew Bennett and his team of researchers have pioneered much of the approach we have taken and have been an inspiration in the field of restoration ecology and wildlife conservation in rural landscapes.

Contents

What is wildlife habitat? 1

Why conserving wildlife on your property is important 1

What is wildlife habitat? 2

Habitat is complex 6

Why does this book focus on habitat? 6

Habitat 1: Trees 10

Trees and hollows 10

Food for animals—leaves, flowers, seeds, sap and bark 12

Trees and mistletoe 14

The importance of stands of trees 14

Farm management for trees 16

Habitat 2: Understorey trees and shrubs 18

Understorey trees and shrubs as feeding and nesting places 18

Understorey trees, noisy miners and the 'health' of bushland 20

Farm management for understorey trees and shrubs 21

Habitat 3: Logs, surface rocks and ground cover 22

Logs and fallen branches as animal habitat 22

Surface rocks as animal habitat 25

Native grassland habitats 25

Farm management for logs, surface rocks and ground cover 26

Habitat 4: Creeks, wetlands and dams 28

Management for creeks, wetlands and dams 30

Integrating farm management and wildlife conservation   34

Wildlife conservation as part of farm management   35

Funding and assistance to promote wildlife conservation   39

Restoring habitat for wildlife   40

Controlling introduced predators   41

Controlling domestic cats   43

Managing other people who come on to your land   43

Planning roads and tracks   43

Animals and the habitats they need   44

Trees

Squirrel glider   46

Koala   48

Brush-tailed phascogale   50

Swift parrot   52

Glossy black-cockatoo   54

Sacred kingfisher   56

Lace monitor   58

Carpet python   60

Peron's tree frog   62

Understorey trees and shrubs

Common ringtail possum   64

Rufous whistler   66

Scarlet robin   68

Logs, rocks and ground cover

Yellow-footed antechinus   70

Echidna   72

Brown treecreeper   74

Bush stone-curlew   76

Diamond firetail   78

Olive legless lizard   80

Southern rainbow skink   82

Marbled gecko   84

Cunningham's skink   86

Green and golden bell frog   88

Creeks, wetlands and dams

Platypus   90

Common eastern froglet   92

Spotted marsh frog   94

Striped marsh frog   96

Bibron's toadlet   98

Smooth toadlet   100

Booroolong frog   102

Glossary   104

General reading   106

Scientific literature   108

Index   113

Reader feedback   118

What is wildlife habitat?

Watching a scarlet robin as it swoops on an insect or the acrobatic flight of a sugar glider is a wonderful experience. You don't need to travel to a remote national park or an inaccessible wilderness to see these natural wonders. Scarlet robins, sugar gliders and many other native animals live on farms in south-eastern Australia. The presence of suitable habitat—that is places where animals can find food, shelter and are able to breed—is the main reason why a particular species occurs on a particular property. For this reason, the conservation of habitats is the key to conserving wildlife.

This book is about types of habitats found on farms and some of the mammals, birds, reptiles and frogs that use them. We discuss how modified farm management practices used in running profitable farming businesses can have a positive impact on native animals. Simple changes to activities such as firewood collection, burning or spraying may protect these habitats and help people on the land make a major contribution to wildlife conservation.

Why conserving wildlife on your property is important

The chances are, if you are reading this book, that you probably already think that wildlife conservation is important. Four good reasons why this is so particularly applicable to farms are listed below.

• New financial incentive schemes are presently being developed which aim to pay people on the land to maintain values such as wildlife conservation. Landholders who already have properties with good quality habitat for wildlife will be in a strong position to access these sorts of funds.

• Some species of native animals and the conservation of native vegetation can contribute to the productivity of farms and agricultural ecosystems (see box on page 2). This can improve the profitability of farm enterprises.

• Vegetation types like yellow box/white box woodlands and native grasslands are found almost exclusively on private land and are not well represented in national parks and reserves.

Native wildlife and farm productivity

Some species of native animals can contribute to farm productivity. For example, birds and gliders pollinate many plants and help to control insect pests. A sugar glider, a close relative of the squirrel glider featured on page 46, may eat 25 Christmas beetles per day. These insects are serious pests on eucalypt trees. A colony of sugar gliders (comprising up to eight animals) may consume more than 200 kg of beetles each year. The decline in sugar gliders may be one of the causes of eucalypt dieback.

Honeyeaters and other birds also eat insect pests, and may eat up to 60% of insects found on woodland trees.

Mike Greer/Chicago Zoological Society

An ibis eats up to 250 g of pasture insects each day and the Australian magpie can consume large numbers of damaging scarab beetle larvae. Larger reptiles such as the lace monitor (goanna) and carpet python eat pests such as mice and rabbits.

The conservation of habitats (and the animals associated with them) in these types of vegetation depends on sympathetic management of private land.

• Wildlife is a part of bush culture, and for many people on the land it contributes to the quality of rural life. Wildlife is also part of Australia's natural heritage. Older people have seen many bush creatures such as the bush stone-curlew and platypus decline or disappear. It would be a shame if the next generations of Australians could not experience the wildlife that we presently enjoy.

What is wildlife habitat?

Habitat is *the environment in which a species can occur, survive and reproduce.*

Habitat for wildlife means much more than just trees and in this book we look at four broad habitat types:

• Big trees, both living and dead ones

• Understorey trees and shrubs

• Logs, rocks and groundcover such as native grasses

• Creeks, rivers, and wetlands.

Tree and understorey habitats.

Log and rock habitats.

Native grassland.

A creek system and its associated vegetation.

Artificial structures such as dams and buildings may also provide habitat for some native animals.

We have chosen a set of mammals, birds, reptiles and frogs that depend on each of the four broad types of habitat featured in this book. These animals are shown on the next two pages (pages 4 and 5) and are then described in detail in the second part of this book.

These same four habitats also support many other species not mentioned in this book. Therefore, efforts to conserve these habitat types will benefit many more animals than just the ones described here.

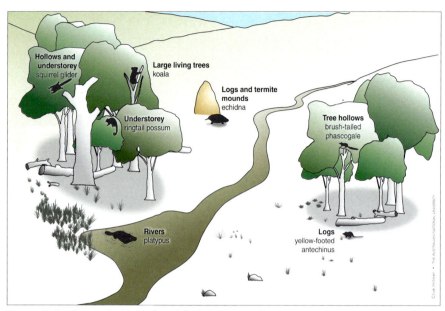

Mammals that feature in this book and the habitats used by them.

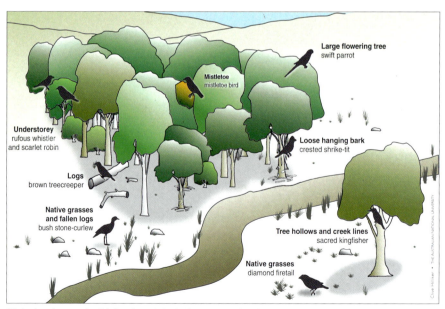

Birds that feature in this book and the habitats used by them.

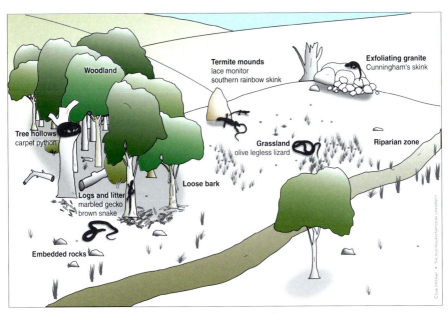

Reptiles that feature in this book and the habitats used by them.

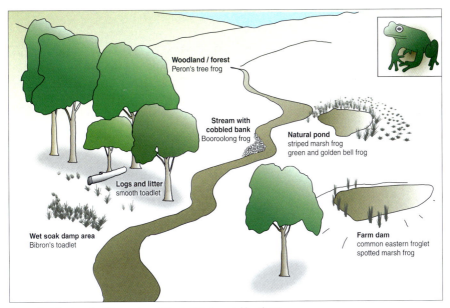

Frogs that feature in this book and the habitats used by them.

Habitat is complex

Even a quick look at the birds and animals in this book will reveal two important facts. First, most animals are dependent on more than one type of habitat—the squirrel glider, for example, needs large hollow trees for nesting *and* understorey trees for feeding (see page 46). Logs and rocks are key habitats for many reptiles, but tree hollows and vegetation on the ground are also critical. The animals that depend on rivers, creeks, wetlands and dams may also need other types of habitat. Frogs are a classic example. Out of the breeding season, when frogs are silent, they may move away from water in search of shelter under rocks, in cracks in the soil, under logs, in tree hollows, at the base of tussocks and even in garden beds around farmhouses.

Second, different species need different habitats: a glossy black-cockatoo (see page 54) needs she-oak trees for food, while the swift parrot (see page 52) forages among the blossoms of large winter-flowering eucalypts and wattles. Because different birds and animals need different habitats, it is possible for many different species to coexist. Places with varied vegetation (for example, areas with tall trees, shrubs and ground cover) have a greater diversity of wildlife than places where the structure of the vegetation is simple and has fewer layers (see the figure opposite). Fewer layers contain fewer habitats. The same is true of places with a variety of creeks, dams and ground habitats—more species are likely to occur there.

Why does this book focus on habitat?

This book focuses on habitats for several good reasons. First, habitat loss is the main reason why birds and animals have declined or become extinct all over the world. Conserving habitat and conserving wildlife are therefore closely intertwined.

Second, you can only conserve a species and increase its chances of survival if you understand the habitat that it needs. For this reason, we suggest ways of protecting habitats for each species including the integration of conservation measures with normal farm management practices.

Third, creating new habitats with revegetation programs is difficult and slow. It may be 200 years before this year's tube-stock is big enough for rosellas to nest in. Restored habitats are never as good as the original ones. It is much more important, economical and timely, to save existing habitats than to create new ones. (Revegetation is discussed later in this section.)

In this book we emphasise the importance of local habitat features: a stand of big old trees, a rock pile or a fallen hollow log. For some wildlife species, it is not just one local feature, but the total amount of vegetation within several hundred metres or several kilometres, that may be the critical factor. For example, large areas of bush (20–200 ha), are significant for wildlife because they may support more types of habitat and therefore more

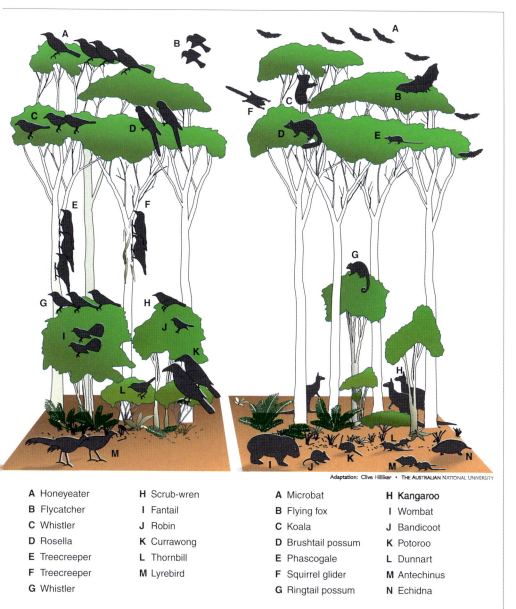

A Honeyeater	**H** Scrub-wren	**A** Microbat	**H** Kangaroo
B Flycatcher	**I** Fantail	**B** Flying fox	**I** Wombat
C Whistler	**J** Robin	**C** Koala	**J** Bandicoot
D Rosella	**K** Currawong	**D** Brushtail possum	**K** Potoroo
E Treecreeper	**L** Thornbill	**E** Phascogale	**L** Dunnart
F Treecreeper	**M** Lyrebird	**F** Squirrel glider	**M** Antechinus
G Whistler		**G** Ringtail possum	**N** Echidna

Adaptation: Clive Hilliker • THE AUSTRALIAN NATIONAL UNIVERSITY

Typical woodland showing how different species of mammals and birds relate to different layers. The diagram illustrates why areas of complex habitat with many layers support more species (based on a drawing in Woinarski *et al.*, 1997).

Christopher MacGregor

Remnant vegetation is broadly defined as any area of native vegetation—including stands of regrowth sapling trees, shrubs or native grasslands.

species, including rare or unusual ones. This does not mean that smaller areas are unimportant—many native animals use even tiny remnants of bushland and these too should be conserved wherever possible. Nevertheless, we have not discussed *how much* habitat is needed for a particular species because this subject is still poorly understood. (More detailed useful information can be found in publications such as *How to Plan Wildlife Landscapes* by S. Platt.)

Although we focus on south-eastern Australia, many of the birds and other animals we describe are also found outside this region. For this reason, the farm management practices discussed below will be relevant in other parts of Australia. However, we recognise that in some places such as extensive and

intensive grain cropping areas, different sorts of strategies to the ones outlined in this book will be required.

Important caveats
This book is based on the best available knowledge we have been able to gather on the mammals, birds, reptiles and frogs that may occur on private land in south-eastern Australia. However, we would emphasise that a lot is still not known about the best ways to conserve, create and manage the habitats they need. For example, wildlife use of cropped areas, pastures and fallow paddocks on farms has received very limited study. Nevertheless, there is presently an enormous scientific effort targeted at better understanding habitat conservation and integrating it with

farm management. As this new knowledge becomes available, we hope it can be used to assist people on the land conserve habitat and hence wildlife as part of their management practices.

The word 'science' comes from the Latin word *scientia* meaning 'knowledge'. Many landholders have vital knowledge in that they have an enormous body of hands-on expertise and information that we may have missed or overlooked in writing this book. We are keen to get feedback so future editions can be improved to better assist landholders integrate wildlife conservation with farm management practices. We would greatly appreciate receiving your comments— please see page 118 for our contact details.

In summary

The main message of this book is that the conservation of habitats is the key to the conservation of native birds and other animals. Habitat is not just trees—many other features, from shrubs and logs to creeks and wetlands, are also critical. Despite the value of revegetation programs, it is much better to conserve existing habitats than to lose them and try to re-create them later. Perhaps the most important point is that there are many (sometimes quite simple) ways in which people on the land may make a substantial contribution to providing habitat and conserving native wildlife while still running profitable and sustainable farming businesses.

David Lindenmayer

In some areas of south-eastern Australia, such as the south-west slopes of New South Wales and south-east South Australia, paddock trees comprise a significant proportion of the remaining vegetation cover. They can provide valuable habitat for many species of native animals.

Habitat 1: Trees

Trees are important on properties: they have aesthetic value, provide shelter for stock, and they may prevent soil erosion and rising watertables. Large trees can act as windbreaks and contribute to pasture improvement and/or enhanced stock condition in the adjacent paddocks. Native trees are one of the most conspicuous types of wildlife habitat on farms. They are vital for attracting wildlife, and provide places for many animals to feed, shelter and breed. Not all trees, however, have equal habitat value. Big old trees are particularly important. Research by Birds Australia has shown that the number of bird species on a property increases by 30% for every 10 large trees.

More information is presented in this book on trees than the three other broad types of habitat. This is for two key reasons. First, more is known about the importance of trees for wildlife than the other types of habitat. Second, trees contribute to habitat quality in all four types of habitat we identify in this book—as large standing living and dead trees, as saplings in part of the understorey, as fallen logs and branches as well as seedlings and very young plants on the ground, and finally as

David Lindenmayer

Dead trees provide important habitat for a wide range of native animals on farms. For example, they are perching and calling places for many types of native birds including woodswallows, eastern rosellas, rainbow bee-eaters and dollarbirds.

submerged and partially submerged trees in creeks and wetlands.

Trees and hollows

Large trees often contain hollows that are critical to the survival of over 300 species (or more than 15%) of

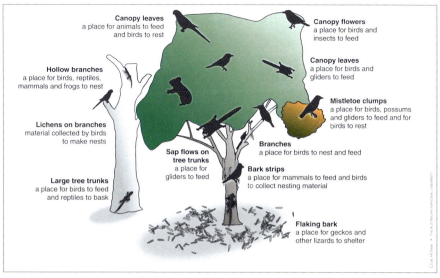

Canopy leaves
a place for animals to feed
and birds to rest

Canopy flowers
a place for birds and
insects to feed

Hollow branches
a place for birds, reptiles,
mammals and frogs to nest

Canopy leaves
a place for birds and
gliders to feed

Mistletoe clumps
a place for birds, possums
and gliders to feed and for
birds to rest

Lichens on branches
material collected by birds
to make nests

Sap flows on
tree trunks
a place for
gliders to feed

Branches
a place for birds to nest and feed

Bark strips
a place for mammals to feed and birds
to collect nesting material

Large tree trunks
a place for birds to feed
and reptiles to bask

Flaking bark
a place for geckos and
other lizards to shelter

The wide range of roles played by large trees for native animals.

A hollow woodland tree. The entrance of hollows where animals frequently enter and exit is often smooth and stained by oils deposited from constant brushing by animal feathers or fur.

Australian native vertebrates. They depend on hollows for nesting, sheltering or for finding food. Many people are unaware that dead trees with hollows are just as important for many native animals as live ones. Bats, birds, possums, gliders and reptiles shelter and breed in dead hollow trees.

Hollows start developing in a tree as a result of natural events that damage the trunk or branches like fires and windstorms or mistletoe infections. Termites, fungi and bacteria then invade the 'wound site' and promote the decay of wood. This makes the process of hollow formation very slow, and if they are lost, trees with hollows may take more than 100 years to replace. Big old trees with hollows can be protected by fencing out stock, either permanently or temporarily. This will promote the natural regeneration of seedlings—the next cohort of hollow trees.

Pros and cons of nest boxes

Because natural hollows take so long to form, artificial ones like nest boxes can sometimes be used to help conserve animals that depend on hollows. However, nest boxes are inferior to natural hollows, require a lot of maintenance, and may even spread pests such as the introduced starling. Nevertheless, nest boxes are useful if they are carefully designed to meet the specific needs of particular species (see *The Nestbox Book* by J. Grant for a range of designs). For example, the brush-tailed phascogale (see page 50) and the glossy black-cockatoo (see page 54) are known to occupy specially constructed nest boxes. In these cases, they need entrances to exclude competitors for hollows like feral bees and common brushtail possums.

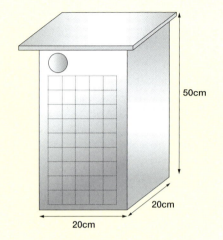

A nest box designed for sugar gliders—the world's most widely distributed marsupial. A ladder of wire mesh or cut steps on the inside will allow the young to climb out. The sugar glider is known to readily occupy nest boxes (redrawn from Grant, 1997).

Food for animals—leaves, flowers, seeds, sap and bark

The leaves of trees are a source of food for a wide range of animals. The koala (see page 48), for example, feeds almost entirely on eucalypt leaves—especially those of manna gum and narrow-leaved peppermint that are particularly nutritious. The leaves of eucalypt trees are also eaten by a huge number of native insects. These are, in turn, eaten by birds and mammals. Sap-sucking insects called lerps produce a white sugary covering on eucalypt leaves and these are food for gliders and birds such as the spotted pardalote.

Big, old eucalypts often flower profusely and are major sources of pollen and nectar. The number of flowers on large 200-year-old trees may be up to 15

Lerp on eucalypt leaves—a valuable food source for many birds and mammals. The removal of lerp by animals is important otherwise heavy infestations can cause dieback.

times greater than on 20-year-old saplings. Large trees also provide more reliable and consistent sources of nectar and pollen than smaller ones, and they are actively sought out by insects, gliding possums, bats and birds.

Large trees are a valuable source of sap for the sugar and squirrel gliders. Sugar gliders use their large lower incisors to tap the trunks of eucalypt trees to obtain sap. The marks they leave are a useful sign of their presence. Trees tapped by gliders tend to have higher rates of sap flow than others in a stand. Sap sites are changed frequently because the wounds 'heal' within a few weeks, so that gliders no longer use them.

As they mature and grow, many eucalypts (such as ribbon or manna gum) shed long straps of peeling bark from their trunks and branches. Some trees shed as much as one tonne of bark per year. Bark strips provide shelter for insects and spiders, many of which are predators of pest insects. The tiny animals that live in bark are also eaten by birds and mammals. Fallen bark and leaf litter are foraging areas and shelter sites for animals such as skinks and geckos (see pages 82, 84). Bark has many other roles. For example, the common ringtail possum (see page 64) as well as

Mason Crane

A large flowering ironbark—an important winter-flowering tree for many birds and mammals living on farms.

many native birds, such as the noisy friarbird and the scarlet robin, use bark strips to build their nests. Many species of eucalypts have bark that does not form long strips but rather remains

Bark strips and the crested shrike-tit

The crested shrike-tit often searches for food on strips of bark that hang from trees such as ribbon gum. Peeling back the bark is a noisy activity which means they are often heard before they are seen. The shrike-tit's bill is powerful and slightly hooked—adaptations to its bark-stripping habits. Although it is moderately common in some forest areas, it is now uncommon or rare in many woodlands, possibly because of the declining numbers of large trees.

Ian R McCann/Nature Focus

attached to the tree trunk. These too can be valuable habitats for animals—for example, woodswallows often make their nests in these sorts of places.

Many species of trees produce seeds eaten by native animals. For example, the glossy black-cockatoo feeds primarily on the seeds of she-oak, and eucalypt seeds are eaten by parrots and cockatoos (e.g. the gang-gang cockatoo).

It is not only living trees that are important places for animals to find food. After a tree dies, wood-boring insects may colonise it to feed on the decaying wood. Brown treecreepers, which feed on insects in dead wood, are usually found where there are dead trees.

Trees and mistletoe

More than 20 species of native mistletoes occur in eastern Australia. Although they are parasites on eucalypts, casuarinas and other plants, they are habitat for many animals in rural landscapes. The dense foliage of mistletoes provides good nesting sites for many birds such as noisy friarbirds and leaden flycatchers. Mistletoe produces abundant nectar, fruit, and seeds that are eaten by many species of birds and animals including the mistletoe bird (see the box below). The leaves of mistletoes are food for mammals such as the common ringtail possum.

The importance of stands of trees

Big old trees provide habitat for the greatest range of animals when they occur in association with other trees. This is why larger areas of remnant vegetation, especially those that exceed several hectares, are often the most valuable ones for wildlife. Nevertheless, smaller areas, and even individual trees, are valuable. In some landscapes, small areas of native vegetation are all that remain. Even if you only have scattered paddock trees, they are important habitat and are worth looking after.

Mistletoe and the mistletoe bird

The mistletoe bird specialises in eating the fruit of mistletoes and is largely responsible for dispersing these parasitic plants. Two other species of birds (the painted honeyeater and the spiny-cheeked honeyeater) also feed on mistletoes. The seeds pass through the gut of these birds and are deposited on a branch where they germinate. Like many species of birds, the male mistletoe bird is the more colourful of the sexes. The striking red throat is particularly distinctive. Its call is a rapid and high-pitched 'tee-pee, tee-pee, tee-

Roger Brown/Auscape

pee'. Females are a similar size but are not brightly coloured—which is perhaps a strategy to not draw attention to them when they are sitting on the nest.

Paddock trees

A ring of seedlings will often regenerate around a large paddock tree where grazing pressure has been eased—even temporarily. These are important places where the next cohort of trees on a farm can develop. Paddock trees have many other vital roles: they reduce soil erosion from both wind and water, limit the loss of soil nutrients, and can prevent watertables from rising.

Areas of remnant vegetation do not have to be large to be valuable for wildlife—many birds and animals feed and nest in isolated paddock trees.

David Lindenmayer

Paddock trees also provide 'stepping stones' for birds and bats moving from place to place.

Damian Michael

Eucalypt tree supporting many clumps of mistletoe. Although mistletoe is a very important resource for many animals, large numbers of this parasitic plant can kill the host tree. One way to improve the health of a heavily infested tree is to remove some (but not) all mistletoes by using a cherry-picker to cut them down. It can be useful to leave the cuttings on the ground as they provide nutrient-rich leaf litter. In other cases, specific herbicides injected into the trunk of the tree can help control mistletoe numbers.

Farm management for trees

It is critical to preserve any existing trees for wildlife on farms, especially large ones with hollows. This is because it takes a very long time (sometimes many hundreds of years) for new trees to develop the same characteristics that make old trees so valuable for many animals. This includes large dead trees with hollows that may provide nesting sites. It is important to avoid felling dead trees (e.g. for firewood) wherever possible. Because dead trees are such valuable wildlife habitat, it may be best to restrict access to your land by firewood contractors, or at least limit their activities to certain areas.

In addition to standing living and dead trees being critical habitats, large tree stumps can also be valuable for many animals. They can be used for foraging and basking by geckos and other lizards and the exposed hollow centre can provide nesting sites for birds such as the grey shrike-thrush and the turquoise parrot. If trees have to be cut down on a farm, try and leave the stumps behind rather than pulling them out.

Large eucalypt trees eventually die and collapse to the ground (where they have valuable roles as log and fallen timber habitats—see pages 22–24), and so it is essential to have young trees growing up to replace them. Fencing off areas of remnant vegetation protects the trees and reduces grazing pressure. This will enable natural regeneration to occur. A recent study found that more than 90% of unfenced woodlands in southern New South Wales had no regenerating trees. When fencing woodland remnants it may be worthwhile to use plain wire

David Lindenmayer

Tree stumps left after felling trees can be very useful foraging and nesting sites for many animals. These stumps are used by turquoise parrots.

on the top one or two strands. This is because gliders may become entangled in barbed wire and die.

Paddock trees may be protected with wire cages to exclude stock. The extra nutrients in the dung of cattle and sheep that accumulates around unfenced paddock trees provides ideal conditions for flushes of insects. These, in turn, make paddock trees more susceptible to insect damage and dieback.

As an adjunct to encouraging natural regeneration, planting tube-stock is a popular way to ensure that new trees will replace old ones that die. However, replanting is more expensive and generally less successful than natural regeneration.

The most appropriate revegetation schemes for wildlife are those that attempt to recreate the vegetation cover that existed before the land was cleared. For this reason it is important to plant local species—although in some cases it may be essential to plant exotic trees around a homestead to minimise fire risks.

If you are interested in revegetation and these trees do occur naturally in your area, then species that flower heavily in winter such as red ironbark and golden wattle are valuable for rosellas, honeyeaters, silvereyes and the swift parrot (see page 52). She-oaks are excellent trees to use in replanting and revegetation programs and local species of *Allocasuarina* and *Casuarina* should eventually benefit the glossy black-cockatoo (see page 54).

Mal Baker

A greater glider entangled in a barbed wire fence. Using plain wire on the top strands of a fence may reduce this problem. Although this may make fences ineffective for some domestic stock (particularly cattle), electric fencing can overcome this problem.

If you have a farm forestry project on your land, another way to grow large trees is to exempt some of them from harvesting and allow them to grow to maturity.

Finally, the prudent use of fire is important for preserving remnant vegetation and encouraging the growth of large trees. Wherever possible try to avoid high-intensity fires as these kill both young and old trees. High-intensity crown fires are also known to kill native animals such as the koala.

Habitat 2: Understorey trees and shrubs

Understorey trees and shrubs, such as wattles and tea-trees, play many key roles on farms. They provide wind protection and slow or stop the loss of leaf litter. As in the case of large trees, understorey trees and shrubs stabilise the soil and limit soil erosion. Wattles help fix nitrogen and accelerate the growth of other plants such as eucalypt trees. This is why mixed plantings in shelter belts and other revegetation areas are more successful than single species plantings. Understorey trees and shrubs are also very valuable for wildlife.

Understorey trees and shrubs as feeding and nesting places

Many kinds of birds and other animals prefer to feed in understorey trees and shrubs rather than foraging in open areas where they can be vulnerable to predators. The leaves of wattle trees support insects that are eaten by gliders and birds. Wattle seeds are consumed by large native pigeons such as the common bronzewing. Some species of wattle trees (such as black wattle) produce nodules of sap or gum eaten by gliders as well as honeyeaters. Wattle gum is produced by trees in response to physical damage to the trunks and branches. Sugar and squirrel gliders chew holes in the bark to stimulate gum flow. These distinctive marks are a telltale sign that a colony of gliders lives nearby. Flowers on correas, grevilleas and other types of understorey plants produce pollen and nectar for insects and birds such as eastern spine-bills and other honeyeaters. Fruits and berries on understorey trees and shrubs (e.g. geebungs) are eaten by many animals (such as possums and emus). The foliage of understorey trees and shrubs is an important food resource for species like the common ringtail possum and the red-necked wallaby.

Wattles and other understorey trees are often attacked by large wood-boring grubs. These are favourite food of black-cockatoos. They use their powerful bills to extract the grubs from deep inside tree trunks. Black-cockatoo fledglings are extremely noisy, squawking incessantly as they beg their parents for these protein-rich larvae.

Understorey trees and shrubs provide places for birds and animals to nest and find shelter—young nestling birds (such as the eastern yellow robin, yellow-rumped thornbill and red-browed firetail) often hide in the understorey.

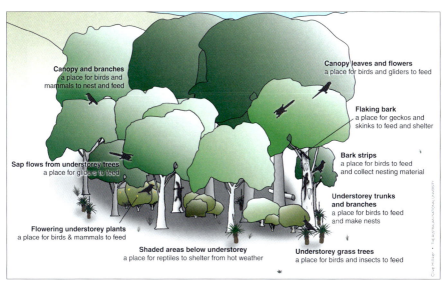

Canopy and branches
a place for birds and mammals to nest and feed

Canopy leaves and flowers
a place for birds and gliders to feed

Flaking bark
a place for geckos and skinks to feed and shelter

Bark strips
a place for birds to feed and collect nesting material

Sap flows from understorey trees
a place for gliders to feed

Understorey trunks and branches
a place for birds to feed and make nests

Flowering understorey plants
a place for birds & mammals to feed

Shaded areas below understorey
a place for reptiles to shelter from hot weather

Understorey grass trees
a place for birds and insects to feed

The wide range of roles played by understorey trees and shrubs for native animals.

Both the understorey vegetation and larger trees provide cover for wildlife during the heat of the day and when it is raining. Common ringtail possums also build stick and leaf nests (called 'dreys') in dense understorey shrubs.

Understorey trees and shrubs benefit farm productivity in obvious ways, such as stabilising the soil, but they also contribute in other unexpected ways. A classic example centres around the swamp (or black) wallaby. It is often

The amazing acacia

Acacias (or wattles) can be significant understorey trees or shrubs in many parts of Australia and are perhaps some of the country's most extraordinary plants. So far, over 950 species of wattles have been described in Australia—making acacia the largest and most diverse genus on the continent. The leaves, flowers, seeds and sap of wattles is food for a huge array of insects, mammals and birds—such as the swift parrot, shown here. Many species make their nests in wattle trees. From a farm productivity perspective, wattle trees have special types of

bacteria that form nodules on the roots and fix nitrogen from the atmosphere. This nitrogen is not readily available to the vast majority of other organisms but is returned to the soil by acacia trees.

found where there is a dense under-storey which provides refuge from introduced predators, such as the fox.

Understorey trees, noisy miners and the 'health' of bushland

Overstorey eucalypts are often in a healthier condition and show fewer signs of dieback where there is an understorey. Bird populations are also significantly larger in areas where dieback is less acute.

The lack of an understorey in an area of bushland can upset normal interactions between different species of animals and even threaten the bushland viability. This has been well documented in the case of the noisy miner; a native but highly aggressive honeyeater.

Mason Crane

Dieback in a eucalypt tree can be the result of any one or a combination of factors ranging from insect attack, rising watertables, and simply a tree becoming old and beginning to senesce and eventually die.

Understorey trees, swamp wallabies and farm productivity

The swamp wallaby has an extraordinary ecological role in many habitats because at certain times of the year it eats underground fruiting fungi known as native truffles. These fungi germinate after passing through the gut of the wallaby. The newly developing fungi attach themselves to the roots of trees and other plants, and form a mutually beneficial or symbiotic relationship with them. The fungus is essential for plants because it takes up water and nutrients and transfers them to the host plant. The presence of these fungi is one of the reasons why eucalypts grow in the poor soils characteristic of many parts of Australia. They also protect the host plant from soil pathogens, such as

Esther Beaton

cinnamon fungus, which may cause dieback. In return, truffles receive energy from the host in the form of carbohydrates. Retaining understorey vegetation for swamp wallabies and other truffle-eating animals will allow this complex cycle to function freely and will benefit the establishment, vigour and growth of larger trees.

The noisy miner and understorey trees and shrubs

The noisy miner is a loud-calling bird that lives in loose colonies of up to 30 individuals. It can be extremely common in many areas of woodland throughout much of eastern Australia, particularly in areas without an understorey. Being strongly territorial, noisy miners chase away most other smaller insect-eating birds. The reduction in the number of insectivorous species may leave eucalypt trees susceptible to dieback through overgrazing by insects. The negative effects of noisy miners on other birds are clear from studies of woodlands where miners have been removed: smaller birds quickly return. This indicates a strong case for noisy miner control on many farms.

Esther Beaton

Several strategies help limit some of the problems created by noisy miners. First, populations are markedly lower in remnant vegetation with a well-developed understorey layer, so encouraging understorey regeneration is useful. Second, as miners prefer to live on the edges of remnant vegetation, conserving larger areas of remnant vegetation will ensure there is habitat deeper inside for other species of birds.

Farm management for understorey trees and shrubs

You can protect the understorey and stimulate its natural regeneration by controlling (but not always reducing) grazing pressure. The best time to graze areas supporting sensitive plants is after flowering and seed set has occurred so that they can reproduce. Stock rotation may also promote natural regeneration. In some cases, it may be necessary to reduce the numbers of kangaroos or rabbits which eat young seedlings. Frequent high-intensity fires may limit the regeneration of some important understorey trees and shrubs such as she-oaks. Low-intensity or hazard reduction burns that are restricted to the boundaries of paddocks will not have such a great impact on regenerating vegetation.

Replanting understorey vegetation is another strategy that may have major benefits for wildlife. For example, certain types of wattles are useful for many species, not only abundant ones such as rosellas but also uncommon animals like the squirrel glider. The value of planting wattles may be increased if they are established near stands of large overstorey eucalypt trees with hollows or near eucalypts which flower heavily. It can be useful to visit patches of remnant vegetation in your region for ideas on the types of understorey trees and shrubs to establish.

Habitat 3: Logs, surface rocks and ground cover

Logs, fallen branches, leaf litter, piles of rocks and boulders, natural cracks in the soil and ground cover plants (including native grasses, orchids and native daisies) provide critical habitats for many small mammals, birds, reptiles and frogs. In forest environments, 20% of all animal species rely on dead wood in fallen logs or standing trees. Logs are just as important in woodland environments.

Logs and fallen branches as animal habitat

Logs and fallen branches have an array of roles for wildlife.

- Breeding and sheltering sites: many reptiles including skinks and geckos lay their eggs inside or underneath logs. In addition, species ranging from frogs to echidnas, shelter in hollows in fallen trees.

Mason Crane

Areas with ground cover plants are often very valuable sheltering places for many native animals ranging from marsupial mice (antechinuses—see page 70) to frogs and skinks.

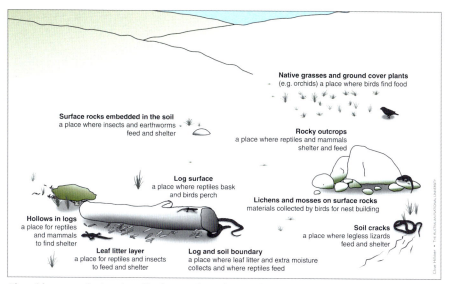

Native grasses and ground cover plants
(e.g. orchids) a place where birds find food

Surface rocks embedded in the soil
a place where insects and earthworms
feed and shelter

Rocky outcrops
a place where reptiles and mammals
shelter and feed

Log surface
a place where reptiles bask
and birds perch

Lichens and mosses on surface rocks
materials collected by birds for nest building

Hollows in logs
a place for reptiles
and mammals
to find shelter

Soil cracks
a place where legless lizards
feed and shelter

Leaf litter layer
a place for reptiles and insects
to feed and shelter

Log and soil boundary
a place where leaf litter and extra moisture
collects and where reptiles feed

The wide range of roles played by logs, rocks and ground cover for native animals.

- Foraging sites: many groups of insects feed on rotting wood inside logs. These are, in turn, sought out by insect-eaters such as the echidna, yellow-footed antechinus and the brown treecreeper.

- Basking and hibernation sites: many species of reptiles bask on logs. Several species of skinks hibernate in communal groups during winter deep inside rotting logs (see box overleaf on basking sites).

- Perching sites: birds perch on (and call from) logs and fallen branches. Seeds passed by these animals while they are perching often germinate in the moist leaf litter and soil that accumulate around logs (see below).

- Runways: many species of ground-dwelling animals such as native rodents and antechinuses (see page 70) use fallen logs and the clear areas directly adjacent to them as runways through the bush.

- Camouflage: species such as the bush stone-curlew (see page 76) shelter and make their nests in areas with many logs, fallen branches and leaf litter.

- Nurseries: logs provide places for plants and fungi to germinate and grow. These include trees, ferns, mosses and liverworts. As the log rots, a tree seedling's root system penetrates the decomposing mulch and extends into the topsoil.

- Natural leaf-litter traps: leaves and soil often accumulate next to fallen logs and branches. Insects and spiders are attracted to these damp and nutrient-rich areas where they shelter and feed. Native animals such as frogs and reptiles then prey on the invertebrates that live in these areas.

Why reptiles need basking sites

Temperature has a great influence on many aspects of the biology of reptiles. It can even influence the sex of the offspring. For example, the water skink produces male young when temperatures are hot. Reptiles are 'cold-blooded' animals and often need the energy of the sun to aid activities such as movement and the digestion of their food. For this reason, they need to bask on logs, rock piles and roads. Many reptiles in south-eastern Australia seek shelter in logs and under rocks during the colder months and are not seen during these times. Temperature explains why reptiles are rarely seen during the heat of a summer day: they hide to avoid the risk of overheating.

Logs contain many nutrients such as carbon and nitrogen. When logs decay, these nutrients enter the soil and contribute to soil fertility and productivity. Logs and leaf litter can slow down the surface flow of water, allowing it to sink in rather than flowing rapidly away. Logs may also retain moisture that is released back into the soil as they decompose. Large populations of smaller animals, such as earthworms, can be associated with the soil in and around logs. These worms free up the soil, improve fertility and ultimately boost paddock productivity. The moisture around logs provides a refuge during dry times for frogs and other animals.

Ground-layer habitats and dangerous native animals: the brown snake

The eastern brown snake is one of the most widely distributed snakes in Australia and is familiar to almost every landowner. The scientific name of the brown snake is *Pseudonaja textilis*. The first part of the name means 'false cobra'—which refers to its cobra-like habit of expanding and flattening its neck when threatened. The brown snake is one of the nation's most dangerous animals and kills more people than any other Australian snake (although deaths from snakebite are rare). Even baby brown snakes have enough venom to kill an adult human. There are simple ways to reduce encounters with the brown snake.

Esther Beaton

One is to remove sheets of iron, piles of cut firewood and other potential shelter sites for snakes situated close to farmhouses and other buildings. A second is to control the numbers of mice around farm buildings. Research on the brown snake has shown that the species is reluctant to attack humans and would rather escape or hide in order to avoid an encounter.

Bushrock, gardens and the loss of native animals

Surface rock piles are a key type of habitat for many species, particularly reptiles but also native invertebrates that are, in turn, sought out by echidnas. Many Australian city-dwellers decorate their gardens with 'bushrock', but few would realise what an impact the removal of rock has on the natural environment. The habitat value of bushrock is often not recognised until those species that depend on it become threatened. One example is the decline of the broad-headed snake. This is a spectacular venomous species that resembles the diamond python because of its broad head and patterned skin. It lives around weathered rocky outcrops in the Hawkesbury Sandstone—an area encompassing about 250 km around

Christopher MacGregor

Sydney. Rocks are taken from this area for use in suburban gardens. The decline of the broad-headed snake as a result of habitat destruction was recognised more than 135 years ago. To overcome the problem, city-dwellers need to be educated in the importance of conserving bushrock as wildlife habitat and encouraged to use quarried rocks in their garden instead of bushrock.

Surface rocks as animal habitat

In addition to fallen logs and branches, surface rocks and piles of boulders are critical habitats for species such as Cunningham's skink (page 86). Rocks embedded in the soil provide animals with protection from predators and a safe place to hide during fires. Surface rocks and logs may also benefit wildlife in indirect ways: the mosses and lichens that form on rocks, for example, are collected by birds such as robins and flycatchers to line their nests. The value of rocky habitats for animals is not always obvious or well recognised. The box above on bushrock demonstrates the conservation problems that may arise when the value of rocky areas is overlooked.

Native grassland habitats

Native grassland is one of the most overlooked and heavily disturbed environments in Australia. Very little native grassland is protected in reserves and much of the grassland that remains has been overtaken by introduced grasses and other plants or heavily modified by grazing and ploughing. This problem is not confined to rural Australia. Significant areas of native grassland are under threat within the boundaries of cities like Canberra— even the new Parliament House was established on an area formerly supporting some important grassland plants—under the noses of Federal environmental policy-makers. Nevertheless, native grassland patches that remain are significant habitats for a number of species. An example is the diamond firetail which eats the seeds of native grasses (see page 78). Others often associated with areas of native grasses and open grassy woodlands include the olive legless lizard (page 80) and the bush stone-curlew—a bird that nests on the ground (page 76).

Farm management for logs, surface rocks and ground cover

There are many approaches to farm management that help to maintain log, surface rock and ground cover habitats. For example, if it is necessary to collect bushrock, then try to limit its removal to paddocks that have already been cleared. It is best to retain bushrock in woodlands and native grasslands.

If there are many logs on the ground and it is necessary to 'tidy-up' to reduce

the risk of fire, hazard-reduction fires can be restricted to the edges of paddocks. It also might be possible to try low-intensity patch burns. These strategies leave some unburnt areas which act as refuges for native plants and animals.

The control of grazing pressure is another useful way of conserving ground-layer habitats. Grazing has a significant impact on species such as the diamond firetail (see page 78) which feeds on the seeds of native grasses. Limiting stock access to woodland remnants may be critical for the bush stone-curlew (see page 76) because their nests may be trampled by livestock.

Because ploughing destroys invertebrate (spider) burrows where animals such as the olive legless lizard shelter and catch their prey, it is a good idea to keep some

Christopher MacGregor

Because logs are such critical habitat but can be significant obstacles for some forms of farm management (like ploughing), if there is a need to move them it may be appropriate to relocate them to areas of remnant woodland.

Christopher MacGregor

An area of native grassland near a fence line where ploughing has not occurred. Ploughing-free areas can be sometimes be retained in places where machinery access may be difficult.

areas unploughed. Also, as heavy applications of fertiliser may destroy some types of native grasslands and lead to the replacement of native perennials and forbs with annuals, it is important to use fertilisers carefully.

Ground-layer habitats may be restored under revegetation programs that include swards of native grasses. It is also possible to create artificial ground-layer habitats with piles of timber offcuts or discarded fence posts. These are useful for species such as the brown treecreeper (see page 74) that use fallen trees. They may also provide shelter and nesting sites for small mammals and reptiles such as geckos and skinks.

David Lindenmayer

A log pile, tin sheets and set of tiles are useful artificial habitats for attracting ground-dwelling reptiles and some species of small native mammals such as dunnarts.

Habitat 4: Creeks, wetlands and dams

Creeks, wetlands and farm dams play a vital role in wildlife conservation even though they usually occupy only a small part of the landscape. Access to water is essential for many animals, especially frogs and waterbirds. Some need drinking-water, others (e.g. the magpie-lark, the white-winged chough and the apostlebird) need mud for building their nests.

The margins of streams and wetlands are critical habitats for many species.

For example, platypus make their burrows in the banks of streams (see page 91), and the Booroolong frog is usually found on cobbled areas of creeks (see page 102).

Trees that have fallen into the water are used by tortoises and water dragons as basking sites. Animals such as fish and yabbies and other invertebrates (which are not covered in detail in this book) rely on creek, wetland and farm dam habitats for their survival. They are also

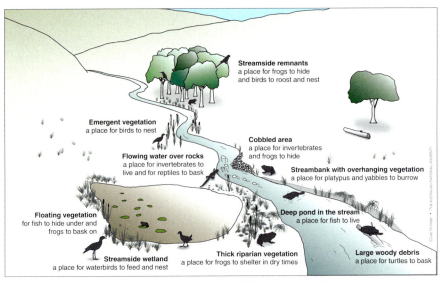

Streamside remnants
a place for frogs to hide
and birds to roost and nest

Emergent vegetation
a place for birds to nest

Cobbled area
a place for invertebrates
and frogs to hide

Flowing water over rocks
a place for invertebrates to
live and for reptiles to bask

Streambank with overhanging vegetation
a place for platypus and yabbies to burrow

Floating vegetation
for fish to hide under and
frogs to bask on

Deep pond in the stream
a place for fish to live

Streamside wetland
a place for waterbirds to feed and nest

Thick riparian vegetation
a place for frogs to shelter in dry times

Large woody debris
a place for turtles to bask

Clive Hilliker • The Australian National University

The wide range of roles played by creeks and wetlands for native animals.

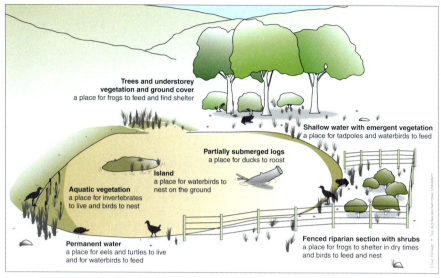

Trees and understorey
vegetation and ground cover
a place for frogs to feed and find shelter

Shallow water with emergent vegetation
a place for tadpoles and waterbirds to feed

Partially submerged logs
a place for ducks to roost

Island
a place for waterbirds to
nest on the ground

Aquatic vegetation
a place for invertebrates
to live and birds to nest

Permanent water
a place for eels and turtles to live
and for waterbirds to feed

Fenced riparian section with shrubs
a place for frogs to shelter in dry times
and birds to feed and nest

The wide range of roles played by farm dams for native animals.

major sources of food for many frogs, reptiles, birds, and mammals. Many birds and animals feed, breed and shelter in the plants around creeks, wetlands and dams (sometimes called 'riparian vegetation').

Plants growing in the water such as emergent vegetation are valuable habitats for frogs and birds and provide shelter and nesting sites for birds like the clamorous reed warbler.

Frogs, farm dams and farm productivity

Farm dams and their associated vegetation are important habitats for frogs. Because frogs live both in water and on land, they can contribute to agricultural ecosystems in several ways. Tadpoles are eaten by yabbies and fish, which on some farms can be harvestable resources. Tadpoles and adult frogs also provide food for waterbirds such as grebes and cormorants that may otherwise target fish that a landholder has intentionally put in a farm dam. As some species of tadpoles are filter feeders, they may influence nutrient levels in the water

that lead to blooms of algae. As adults, frogs feed on small invertebrates such as spiders, beetles and their larvae, flies, mites, earwigs, cockroaches, termites, grasshoppers, crickets, moths and butterflies, millipedes and ants.

Farm dams and increasing native species: the galah and sulphur-crested cockatoo

Esther Beaton

The galah is now far more numerous and widespread than it was at the time of European settlement. Huge flocks of galahs and sulphur-crested cockatoos are common in many parts of south-eastern Australia. The provision of additional water (through the widespread establishment of farm dams) and extra food, particularly seeds from cereal crops and agricultural weeds are thought to have contributed to the population increases and range expansions of both species. Galahs and cockatoos can do considerable damage, particularly to cereal crops. They also compete for tree hollows with other less common parrots and hollow-dependent animals. The cockatoo is also a nuisance in orchards and where crops such as almonds are grown. Netting and scare-guns may be effective deterrents. Revegetation also can deter these birds as it can disrupt the line-of-sight for 'sentinel' members of a flock who watch for approaching predators while the rest of the group is feeding or drinking.

The extra moisture and nutrients from fertile alluvial soils around creeks and gullies stimulate more luxuriant plant growth and may promote the flowering of trees and other plants. This vegetation may support a huge array of invertebrate life. The availability of these extra plant and insect resources is probably why many birds and mammals are more common in vegetation near rivers, streams and water. In other cases, terrestrial animals such as the common ringtail possum (see page 64) produce many more offspring in gullies than on neighbouring ridges. The presence of animals associated with water may have important benefits for farm productivity (see the box opposite on frogs).

Management for creeks, wetlands and dams

A key part of habitat conservation is to avoid draining wetlands and other permanent or semi-permanent waterbodies—access to them is essential for the survival of numerous species of animals and plants. The removal of trees adjacent to these areas will reduce the amount of habitat for many animals. Clearing trees may also cause rising watertables and bring on salinity problems (see *Trees, Water and Salt* by R. Stirzaker *et al.* for a detailed treatment of the complex issues associated with salinity). Salinisation may render creeks, wetlands and dams unsuitable for frogs and other animals.

A severely salt-affected former riparian woodland area in South Australia.

Where possible, it is good to retain trees and to reduce grazing pressure on streambanks. Stock (particularly cattle) access to wetlands and creeks should be controlled, especially when these environments are wet and boggy. Such areas may be managed as a separate paddock, where cattle are 'crash-grazed' during dry times. Installing stock watering points such as farm dams away from rivers also may improve the quality of creek and wetland habitats for wildlife.

You can reduce grazing pressure on creek lines by fencing them off. For example, this may reduce the amount of disturbance of cobbled sections of

Are frogs good 'environmental indicators'?

Many people assume that frogs are good indicators of environmental health and it is certainly better to have some frogs rather than none. Some species of frogs are indeed sensitive to environmental conditions because they may be exposed to toxins both on land and within water and also because they absorb moisture through the skin. However, frogs are not always good indicators of a healthy environment: some species will readily use mud puddles on the roadside and others exist in quite polluted areas. More useful information may be gained by asking questions such as: How many frog species are present? Which species are present? How many species have been lost from the area since European settlement? Are they breeding successfully? Do they show signs of environmental stress, for example, physical deformities like extra, missing or misshapen limbs?

Fencing a patch of remnant vegetation around a creek. This has greatly assisted natural regeneration, although increased numbers of weeds that may occur in these areas can sometimes create management problems.

creeks which provide habitat for the Booroolong frog (see page 102). It also allows vegetation in the water and along the banks to recover.

Sometimes it can be beneficial to fence a farm dam—so as to improve water quality for stock and stop them becoming bogged when it is muddy. When fencing and revegetating part of a farm dam, it is best to focus on the upstream section where the water flows in. This is the area most likely to stay moist during extended dry periods. In addition, once thick vegetation develops it may act as a filter, trapping manure, fertiliser and sediment. Managing direct stock access to dams also benefits frog populations. Cattle sometimes wade into dams to graze on aquatic vegetation which provides protection for frogs.

Managing willows

Willows are an introduced tree and can create problems for some native animals like the platypus—the fibrous root mass of willows makes it difficult for the platypus to dig burrows. Willows are also a hard weed to control. In some cases the best way to manage them is to kill them with stem injections of an appropriate herbicide and then leave them to stand and rot. Wholesale removal of willows in places where they dominate may cause more harm than good. This is because stream environments need some shade to keep water temperature at a suitable level for aquatic life. Too much shade (e.g. from a thick canopy of willows) may also be a problem as aquatic plants need some light to photosynthesise and to replace oxygen in the water. Careful planning is

required to ensure that the benefits of removing willows in a given situation outweigh the benefits of retaining them. State agencies such the New South Wales Department of Land and Water Conservation and the Victorian Department of Sustainability and Environment can help you with these issues and in some cases will need to be contacted for a development application to remove willows.

Burning off in a low-lying swampy area—an activity which can cause long-term damage to these habitats.

Cattle may also disturb egg masses produced by frogs in shallow water.

Some wetland habitats require careful protective management because they can take a long time to replace if they are damaged. A good example is wetlands that contain peat. These may develop over several thousand years but are readily and badly damaged by fire. Fires in peat bogs may dramatically reduce the quality of water within adjacent creeks and also destroy refuge areas that are critical for native animals' survival during droughts.

Maintaining some fish-free farm dams will increase the number of frog species. This is because fish may have a negative impact on the populations of some types of frogs. It is important not to introduce feral mosquito fish to creeks and farm dams because, contrary to popular belief, they do not control mosquito larvae but are major predators of tadpoles and can reduce populations of frogs. Many native fish (such as gudgeons) as well as aquatic invertebrates (such as dragonfly and beetle larvae) better control mosquito larvae.

The use, disposal and leakage of chemicals in water may harm aquatic animals such as the platypus and frogs or the invertebrates on which these animals feed. Even such simple precautions as the careful storage of chemicals and limiting the use of herbicides, weedicides and fertilisers near creeks and during windy weather can reduce the risks of polluting waterways.

Integrating farm management and wildlife conservation

Some farm management practices to promote wildlife conservation have been outlined in the habitat chapters, but there are some practices that relate to several or all the types of habitat that occur on farms. For example, fires may have a significant impact not only on trees and understorey vegetation but also on ground-layer and wetland habitats. Feral predator control is another example—it will benefit animals ranging from those that inhabit creeks and wetlands to large trees. This section examines some conservation-friendly farm management practices, and shows that it is often possible to integrate wildlife conservation with essential farm management activities such as ploughing, burning off, cutting firewood and spraying.

One good way to start integrating farm management and wildlife conservation is to develop a whole-farm plan. This recognises the reality that not all parts of a farm can be managed to maximise conservation objectives. Rather, some places will be more important and others less important—for example, it may prove best to concentrate on habitat conservation on the least productive parts of a farm (thereby having least impact on farm incomes). In other cases, a farm plan may make it possible to graze an area but restrict firewood and bushrock collection to protect log and surface rock habitats. Where there is intensive cropping, it may be impossible to preserve trees, logs and surface rock in paddocks. These parts of a property might be dedicated to intensive cropping and other areas (that are not cropped) managed for a combination of values including wildlife conservation. For these reasons, a whole-farm plan can also help set priorities for deciding which actions would be best applied on what parts of a property—it would be impossible for the vast majority of farmers to do *all* of the things discussed in this book.

Some helpful information on farm planning that includes the conservation of native vegetation is the *Save the Bush Toolkit* by Goldney and Wakefield (available from Charles Sturt University in Bathurst). Another valuable approach is the Potter Farmland Plan. This involves the development of a whole farm plan that considers the nature of the land from agricultural and ecological perspectives (see *Planning for Sustainable Farming: The Potter Farmland Plan Story* by A. Campbell).

There is no simple farm management and conservation planning recipe that can be applied uncritically to every farm. Some activities will be relevant to one farm but not another or may need to be modified to suit particular circumstances. Burning is a good example. The most appropriate fire regimes will depend on the objectives of burning and the vegetation type being burnt—these may be different for a grassy woodland than a native grassland. In many cases you can seek expert guidance on the best ways to tackle these issues (from a Landcare coordinator, an officer from a relevant State Government Agency or a commercial company that specialises in farm planning).

Wildlife conservation as part of farm management

Although there are no generic farm management 'recipes', some general guidelines are:

Preserving existing native vegetation and ground cover
- Wherever possible, preserve existing areas of remnant vegetation including paddock trees, understorey plants, fallen timber and native ground cover.

- If you have to clear some trees or have to cut firewood, try to avoid removing large living and dead trees with hollows—these have special habitat values that take a very long time to replace. If trees have to be cut down, try to leave the stumps—these

Large dead trees can be valuable for many animals on farms. Wherever possible they should not be cut down.

David Lindenmayer

can be useful nesting and foraging habitats for many animals.

- Where possible, leave areas of rocks and boulders intact as they are valuable sheltering and foraging habitat for many animals. If you are going to collect bushrock, try to take it from already cleared paddocks and try not to remove it from woodlands and areas of native grasses.

- Wherever possible, try to maintain tree cover near to creeks, wetlands and farm dams.

Grazing and fencing
- Try to rest patches of native vegetation (and paddock trees) from grazing to promote vegetation recovery and natural regeneration. This also helps to provide habitat for animals that live on the ground. Fencing stock temporarily or permanently out of patches of remnant vegetation can

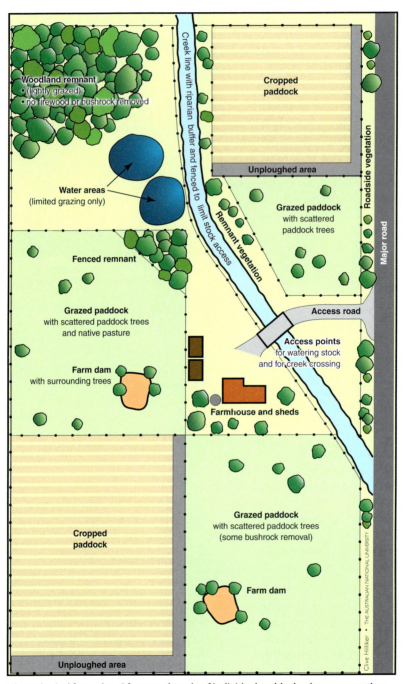

Woodland remnant
• (lightly grazed)
• no firewood or bushrock removed

Creek line with riparian buffer and fenced to limit stock access

Cropped paddock

Unploughed area

Water areas
(limited grazing only)

Remnant vegetation

Grazed paddock
with scattered paddock trees

Roadside vegetation

Major road

Fenced remnant

Grazed paddock
with scattered paddock trees
and native pasture

Access road

Access points
for watering stock
and for creek crossing

Farm dam
with surrounding trees

Farmhouse and sheds

Cropped paddock

Grazed paddock
with scattered paddock trees
(some bushrock removal)

Farm dam

Unploughed area

Clive Hilliker • THE AUSTRALIAN NATIONAL UNIVERSITY

A hypothetical farm plan. Of course the role of individual paddocks changes over time.

Nick Alexander

Fencing of remnant or replanted vegetation is one very significant way to improve the quality of habitats for many native animals.

help rest these areas so that tree seedlings can establish.

- Try to rest native vegetation around creeks, wetlands and farm dams if possible. If these habitats have to be grazed, remember that different domestic livestock have different impacts on regenerating native trees. For example, horses do not eat young eucalypts and sheep do less damage to streambanks and aquatic vegetation than cattle. Sheep are also less likely to cause damage to trees, although they will browse on shrubs.

- If you establish fences around remnant vegetation, try to use plain wire on the top one or two strands. The fence may not be as effective for keeping out domestic stock, but plain wire will reduce the risk of snagging gliding possums and birds.

Ploughing
- Try to maintain some areas on a farm that are not ploughed. Areas of unploughed ground retain a range of key habitat features such as natural soil cracks and invertebrate tunnels.

- When you plough, try to leave an unploughed buffer next to fenced remnants, paddock trees, tree plantings, creeks, wetlands and farm dams. This will limit damage to tree roots and reduce soil erosion and flows of sediment into waterways and dams.

Burning
- When you do hazard reduction burning, try to focus on paddock boundaries, and leave the interior parts unburnt or less intensively burned.

Adrian Manning

Where possible try to avoid burning close to large living and dead paddock trees. Trees with hollows such as this one contain a lot of naturally derived flammable chemicals produced by decaying wood. This makes them especially prone to catching fire which can badly damage them.

- Use low-intensity hazard reduction fires. These have less impact on ground and litter habitats. It is also important that burning-off operations do not become high-intensity crown fires—these may kill animals such as the koala.

- When you need to burn an area, try not to burn all of it at the same time. Rather, apply patchy burns where possible. This has the advantage of providing escape routes for some native animals that would otherwise be killed.

- Where possible, increase the time between burns on the same area to promote the regeneration of native vegetation and allow fire-sensitive species time to recover. For example, in the case of grassy woodlands, the interval between fires should be at least 5–10 years.

- Take care when burning areas near wetlands. If possible, leave an unburnt buffer around wetlands, especially those that contain peat.

Spraying of herbicides, weedicides and fertilisers
- Try to avoid spraying immediately upstream from wetlands and farm dams wherever possible. This helps maintain the quality of the water supply—not only for native animals but also for domestic livestock.

- When you need to spray, try to treat only a few paddocks at a time. Spray-free places may act as refuges for wildlife.

David Lindenmayer

Careful application of chemical sprays can make a significant difference to wildlife populations—some insect-feeding birds like the tawny frogmouth can be quite sensitive to some types of chemicals. Different chemicals have different impacts on wildlife, and all things being equal, try to select the one which has least impact on native animals.

- Try to leave as many years as possible between applications of chemicals to allow animal populations to recover—bird species diversity is higher on farms where fertiliser is applied at intervals longer than five years. In many cases regular spraying is an essential part of a farming business; therefore try to avoid spraying close to remnant vegetation and tree plantings.

Funding and assistance to promote wildlife conservation

Conserving wildlife in rural landscapes can cost money—although the costs can sometimes be offset by increased farm productivity. However, there can be financial losses when landholders set aside parts of a property to conserve remnant vegetation rather than using it for grazing, tree plantations, cropping or producing grapes or olives.

There may also be direct costs associated with rehabilitating habitat for native fauna—erecting fences to protect vegetation, controlling weeds in fenced areas, poisoning introduced predators such as foxes and wild dogs, planting trees and shrubs, and reconstructing wetlands.

Initiatives such as the Commonwealth 'Natural Heritage Trust' have provided funding for conservation programs on private land by community groups. There are also tax concessions available to compensate property owners whose land values may be reduced by setting aside some areas for conservation. There are other support schemes at the

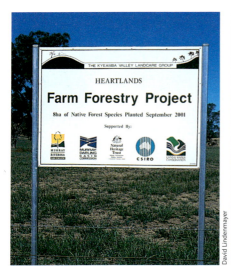

Farm forestry initiatives that assist landholders can be useful ways to both diversify farm income and create habitat for some species of native animals.

Landcare was initially a collaborative idea of the National Farmers Federation and the Australian Conservation Foundation.

State-level, for instance the 'Voluntary Conservation Agreements' administered by the New South Wales National Parks and Wildlife Service. These agreements with the State may allow for a rate reduction as well as funding for the costs of material for activities such as fencing and tree planting. There is also the 'Environmental Services Scheme' run by the New South Wales Department of Land and Water Conservation. This scheme rewards landholders who protect the environment through good land management. It financially supports land-use changes that reduce the threats caused by acid sulphate soils and salinity. 'Bush Tender' is a new program being offered by the Victorian Department of Sustainability and Environment. Landholders receive payment for providing management services that increase the area of native vegetation or improve the quality of native vegetation on their land. Landholders interested in these kinds of schemes should follow up funding opportunities with key organisations such as Greening Australia and Landcare.

Restoring habitat for wildlife

Creating habitat for wildlife is a huge and complex topic and a detailed treatment is well beyond the scope of this book. One of the best sources is *Revegetation and wildlife* by A. Bennett and his colleagues. Generally, the most appropriate revegetation schemes for wildlife are those that attempt to re-create similar types and patterns of vegetation cover that existed in the local area prior to clearing.

It is preferable to plant local species of native trees and shrubs because native

David Lindenmayer

Significant revegetation programs are now well under way in many parts of Australia. It is important to recognise however, that while revegetation programs are valuable, they will never fully re-create the conditions of the original habitat.

birds and animals are more likely to use them than introduced species. For example, local plants will flower at the right time for birds and mammals—as in the case of winter-flowering eucalypts and wattles used by rosellas, honeyeaters and lorikeets, and critical for the survival of the endangered swift parrot.

Areas adjacent to streams and creeks are often the best places to start a restoration program as they typically support large numbers of native animals and can be pathways to help young animals (of some species) disperse to other parts of the landscape. Revegetation in these areas need not focus only on planting trees—ground covers like native tussock grasses, sedges and understorey shrubs (e.g. tea-tree) can be useful to establish.

Controlling introduced predators

The control of introduced predators such as the red fox and wild dogs as well as the feral cat may not only have major benefits for wildlife conservation, but also help reduce stock losses. Many of the animals that feature in this book are susceptible to predation by the red fox and the feral cat; ranging from Peron's tree frog to the brush-tailed phascogale. Packs of wild dogs are also significant predators of native animals (e.g. the swamp wallaby). The feral cat is estimated to be responsible for killing more than 11 million birds a year in Victoria alone. Therefore, poison-baiting programs to destroy pest predators will have positive benefits for many native animals. A number of species have made spectacular

Nature Focus

The enormous populations of red foxes in Australia originated from a small number introduced for sport hunting in southern Victoria. Foxes are able to climb a small distance off the ground and animals such as the common ringtail possum often fall prey to them.

recoveries in places where foxes have been controlled through extensive baiting with 1080 poison. In other cases, like that of the bush stone-curlew, the species remains common in areas such as Kangaroo Island where the red fox was not introduced.

Because foxes and packs of wild dogs are so mobile, baiting programs are more effective if they are coordinated across large areas of a landscape (and therefore over many farms). Officers from the Rural Lands Protection Board (in New South Wales) or the Department of Sustainability and Environment in Victoria can help with concerted baiting programs over large areas to help control foxes. For example, they may recommend burying baits to avoid the accidental poisoning of other

David Lindenmayer

A 1080 poisoning sign.

animals such as the wedge-tailed eagle. Baiting in winter also may be more effective as carrion-feeding animals like the lace monitor (see page 58) are less active at that time and less likely to dig up poison baits.

Controlling domestic cats

Domestic cats kill many native animals on farms. A study in South Australia has shown that household cats (even well-cared-for ones) kill tens of millions of vertebrates each year with each one, on average, killing 30 vertebrates annually. Around the house paddock, Peron's tree frog is particularly vulnerable to predation by the domestic cat. Strategies such as keeping domestic cats inside at night can reduce their impact on native animals.

Mason Crane

A valuable way to protect native wildlife on your land is to control who enters your property and what activities they undertake there. Limiting access to firewood and bushrock contractors or restricting their activities to only certain parts of a farm can be a valuable contribution to wildlife conservation.

Managing other people who come on to your land

Illegal hunting and trapping has had a devastating effect on some native animals; for example, it has reduced populations of the bush stone-curlew. The illegal pet-trade has targeted many species of parrots, cockatoos and other birds as well as lizards and snakes. In the case of animals featured in this book, it has contributed to the decline of the diamond firetail (see page 78) and the carpet python (see page 60).

Planning roads and tracks

If new roads and tracks need to be established on a farm it can be best to build them *around* rather than *through* areas of remnant vegetation. This is because bush tracks, even minor ones, can be barriers to the movement of some animals and fragment and isolate populations living in remaining subdivided native vegetation. In addition, native animals can be killed as a result of collisions with vehicles. The carpet python is an example. It is a slow moving reptile which can be killed or injured on roads or on farmland by heavy vehicles and machinery. Numerous other native animals are killed on roads and tracks ranging from magpies to lizards and frogs.

In summary

There are many things people on the land can do to manage habitats for wildlife. Indeed, landowners *can* make a big difference to conserving the wide range of native animals that occur on farms. Sometimes relatively minor (and inexpensive) changes to farm practices will have large benefits. In other cases more extensive and expensive approaches may be required; but funding is often available from Federal and State schemes.

Animals and the habitats they need

This chapter describes some of the mammals, birds, reptiles and frogs that depend on the four broad types of habitats discussed in this book. The various animals have been assigned to one of the four types based on the habitat feature we believe to be the most likely to be limiting for that species. However, many animals require more than one type of habitat.

Part of the description of each species includes a table outlining some of the things that can be done on a farm to manage its habitat. The strategies are listed in order of priority with those with most ticks (✓✓✓✓) being the most important ones. The last column in the table highlights where in the book further information about how to manage particular habitat features can be found.

Also included in the description for each species is information on some of the key features that can be used in its

identification as well as where it occurs and some of the other common names by which it may be known to landholders. This information is far from exhaustive and readers interested in more details on each of the species covered in this book should refer to the field guides for mammals, birds, reptiles and frogs fully referenced on pages 106–107. The information includes a photograph of the habitat where the species has been found; in virtually all cases the image is from a place where one or more of us has actually seen it. However, it is important for readers to be aware that other sorts of places than those in the habitat photograph may support the species—usually as long as the key habitat features are present.

Some of those chosen are rare such as the bush stone-curlew and the green and golden bell frog. Others like the rufous whistler are quite common. Others may only occur on a seasonal

What you can do on your land	Priority	Page
Preserve large living and dead trees, especially ones with hollows	✓✓✓✓✓	10
Avoid cutting down large dead trees for firewood	✓✓✓✓	35
Preserve understorey trees and shrubs	✓✓	18
Limit the use of barbed wire on the top strands of fences around woodland remnants	✓	17

Habitat for some types of native animals on farms can often be found in some of the least expected places such as: the edge of paddocks (above left), in planted shelter belts between grazed or cropped paddocks (above right), at the edges of farm dams (below).

basis (e.g. the sacred kingfisher) or sporadically such as when large eucalypts are in flower (e.g. the swift parrot). Even if you carefully manage the range of habitats on your land, some of the rarer species of animals may not necessarily return. This may be because all of the populations of that species from your region have disappeared and there are no dispersing animals to recolonise an area of suitable habitat. Nevertheless, careful management of the kinds of habitats featured in this book will be valuable for many other native animals. For example, large hollow trees for the brush-tailed phascogale will be useful for many other hollow-using mammals, birds, reptiles and frogs. Similarly, farm dams managed carefully will be valuable not only for frogs but also will help increase bird species diversity on farms.

Finally, the majority of species in this book are from eastern Australia, particularly the south-eastern part of the continent. This book, however, is not comprehensive—far from it—much more detailed tomes are required to cover the myriad of mammal, bird, reptile and frog species that live in south-eastern Australia. This is only a short, but we hope a practical, guide.

Squirrel glider
Petaurus norfolcensis

The squirrel glider is a medium-sized (40–53 cm) nocturnal gliding possum (170–300 g in weight) that looks very similar to the closely related sugar glider, but is larger (almost twice the size) with a bigger and more thickly furred tail and a white belly. The squirrel glider (like the sugar glider) has a distinct black stripe of fur that starts between the eyes and runs down the back. The tail is sometimes black-tipped but never white-tipped (cf. sugar glider). Both sexes are similar in appearance, although females have a pouch for suckling their young. The squirrel glider is an arboreal (tree-dwelling) marsupial and almost never comes to the ground.

Other common names: Flying squirrel, sugar squirrel, squirrel flying phalanger.

Similar-looking species: Sugar glider (see page 2)

Esther Beaton

Distribution: The squirrel glider has a patchy distribution from western Victoria to northern Queensland (excluding Tasmania). It lives in dry eucalypt forests and woodland as well as paperbark swamps. The species is extinct in South Australia and reports of the species from wet forests in southern coastal New South Wales remain unconfirmed.

Conservation status: The squirrel glider is widespread, generally uncommon, and possibly declining. The species has declined because of clearing of woodlands, firewood collection, as well as inappropriate forms of timber harvesting. Defoliation of trees by insects is also thought to be a factor that might have contributed to the decline of the squirrel glider.

Trees

Key habitat needs: The squirrel glider depends on large trees with hollows for nesting. Nodules of sap produced by wattle trees are an important food source, particularly during winter. Areas with a combination of hollow trees, regenerating eucalypts and understorey wattles are often the most valuable habitats for this species. The species is also often seen in woodlands where several species of eucalypts occur.

Andrew Claridge

Critical features of habitat:
Tree hollows and understorey wattles

What you can do on your land

	Priority	Page
Preserve large living and dead trees, especially ones with hollows	✓✓✓✓✓	10
Preserve native vegetation near creeks, wetlands and farm dams	✓✓✓✓	28
Avoid cutting down large dead trees for firewood	✓✓✓	35
Preserve understorey trees and shrubs	✓✓✓	18
Encourage the natural regeneration of trees, understorey trees and shrubs	✓✓✓	16
Rest areas of native vegetation from grazing	✓✓✓	16
Replant trees and understorey plants	✓✓	40
Control feral predators (and domestic cats)	✓	41
Take care with the construction of roads and tracks	✓	43
Limit use of barbed wire on the top strands of fences around woodland remnants	✓	17

Did you know? Marsupial gliding possums need many different hollow trees to survive. Animals swap frequently between nesting hollows in many different trees. This may be to reduce the chance that predators like owls will discover their nest sites or to try and avoid infestations of fur-living parasitic ticks and fleas.

Koala
Phascolarctos cinereus

Esther Beaton

The koala is a large (75–82 cm) tree-dwelling animal with thick woolly pale-grey to light brown fur. White speckles of fur may occur on the rump. Males are longer and heavier than females. The size and weight of the koala varies substantially throughout the distribution with animals from Queensland being much smaller (male ≈ 7 kg) and shorter than those from Victoria (male ≈ 14 kg). The koala is often seen as a dark immobile 'blob' resting in a tree during the day. When seen in a spotlight at night, the species has a distinctive yellow eyeshine. During the breeding season (spring and summer), male koalas make a loud bellowing or grunting sound reminiscent of a pig.

Other common names: Koala bear, native bear, monkey bear.

Similar-looking species: None.

Distribution: The koala is widely distributed throughout many types of woodland and forest both sides of the Great Dividing Range from far north Queensland to Victoria and South Australia. Populations in some parts of Victoria and South Australia have been established or re-established using animals translocated from islands such as French Island in Westernport Bay (south-west of Melbourne).

Conservation status: The koala was hunted intensively and extensively by both Aboriginal and European Australians. Although the koala is still widespread there are problems with the conservation and management of some populations of the species. The koala is declining as a result of clearing of native vegetation and collisions with motor vehicles in some parts of its range such as coastal New South Wales and Queensland. Elsewhere, such as on Kangaroo Island in South Australia, where an introduced population has been established, there is an over-abundance of animals and trees are suffering dieback from over-grazing by the koala.

Key habitat needs: The diet of the koala is almost exclusively comprised of eucalypt leaves—each animal eats about 500 g of leaves per day. Therefore, stands of eucalypt trees are critical for the survival of the species. Many populations of the koala reach their highest densities in forests and woodlands where the underlying soil is fertile. Trees growing on these soils have high levels of nutrients in their foliage, which is important because the koala depends so heavily on eucalypt foliage. It is for this reason that the koala prefers particular types of trees and in southern Australia these include ribbon gum, blue gum, swamp gum, river red gum, and forest red gum.

Mason Crane

Critical features of habitat:
Eucalypt tree cover on fertile soils

What you can do on your land	Priority	Page
Preserve large living trees	✓✓✓✓✓	10
Encourage the natural regeneration of trees	✓✓✓	16
Rest areas of native vegetation from grazing	✓✓✓	16
Replant trees	✓✓	40
Take care with hazard reduction burning, prevent crown fires from starting	✓	37
Take care with the construction of roads and tracks	✓	43

Did you know? The koala is inactive for up to 20 hours a day. This is because eucalypt leaves contain few nutrients but many toxic chemicals including some with properties not unlike cyanide. Resting for long periods reduces the amount of energy expended by animals and allows them to survive on such a poor diet.

Brush-tailed phascogale

Phascogale tapoatafa

The brush-tailed phascogale is a medium-sized (35–45 cm) nocturnal marsupial (adults weigh 200–300 g). It is a shy and rarely seen animal that spends a large proportion of its active time in trees. It has grey fur above and white to cream-coloured underparts. The species has a highly distinctive black-furred 'bottlebrush' tail with long hairs. Both sexes are similar in appearance (although males are larger and heavier) and females have a pouch for suckling their young. Males die off after mating. Pregnant females carry the next cohort of young males. When animals are agitated, they will often tap their paws on hard surfaces such as branches.

Other common names: Tuan, black-tailed phascogale, common wambenger.

Similar-looking species: Squirrel glider (see page 46), sugar glider (see page 2).

Distribution: The brush-tailed phascogale is widespread but with a patchy distribution. Populations are known from eastern Australia from Victoria to central Queensland, Cape York, Northern Territory and the Kimberley (Western Australia). The brush-tailed phascogale is now believed to be extinct in South Australia. The species is known to occur in dry open eucalypt forest and woodlands.

Conservation status: Uncommon to rare, thought to be declining in large parts of its range due to land clearing, removal of large trees, and the impacts of feral predators.

Key habitat needs: Large trees with hollows are used as nest sites by the brush-tailed phascogale. The species often forages for nectar and insects in large flowering trees.

Todd Soderquist

Trees

Andrew Claridge

Critical features of habitat: Tree hollows and large flowering trees

What you can do on your land

	Priority	Page
Preserve large living and dead trees, especially ones with hollows	✓✓✓✓✓	10
Preserve understorey trees and shrubs	✓✓✓✓	18
Avoid cutting down large dead trees for firewood	✓✓✓	35
Preserve native vegetation near creeks, wetlands and farm dams	✓✓✓	28
Encourage the natural regeneration of trees and understorey trees and shrubs	✓✓✓	16
Rest areas of native vegetation from grazing	✓✓	16
Replant trees and understorey plants	✓	40
Install nest boxes (using a design specifically tailored for the species)	✓	12
Control feral predators (and domestic cats)	✓	41

Did you know? Brush-tailed phascogales produce prodigal sons. Like many mammals, young male brush-tailed phascogales travel a lot further than females when they disperse. Long-distance dispersal in males is a strategy thought to reduce the chance of matings between close relatives. In contrast, young females will often settle very close to where they were born—and in some cases adult females will even give up their own territories to their daughters.

Swift parrot
Lathamus discolor

The swift parrot is a slender green parrot (24 cm in size) with a long dull-red tail and red facial markings. Males and females are similar and have distinctive calls in flight (see below). The species often forms large rapid-flying flocks around large flowering eucalypts.

Other common names: Swift lorikeet, red-shouldered lorikeet, swift-flying lorikeet, swift-flying parakeet, clink, keet, talking keet.

Similar-looking species: Musk lorikeet, little lorikeet.

Voice: Metallic and noisy 'clink-clink' or 'pee-pit, pee-pit' when in flight.

Distribution: The distribution of the swift parrot includes open forests and woodlands in eastern Australia from Tasmania to as far north as central Queensland in some years. The swift parrot breeds in Tasmania in the spring (mostly along the south-east coast of the island). The species is nomadic and migrates during winter to mainland south-eastern Australia.

Conservation status: The swift parrot is uncommon and declining. Clearing of forest and woodland habitat has greatly reduced the number of large flowering trees that are an important source of

Chris Szaros

nectar. In Tasmania, the loss of breeding habitat (such as in swamp gum forest), a reduction of large hollow trees, as well as competition for nest sites from introduced pest birds such as the common starling appear to be influencing populations.

Key habitat needs: In mainland south-eastern Australia, the swift parrot is usually associated with winter-flowering eucalypt trees and wattles that produce abundant nectar (e.g. white box, ribbon gum, grey box, red ironbark and golden wattle).

Damian Michael

Andrew Claridge

Critical features of habitat: Large flowering eucalypts and wattles

What you can do on your land

	Priority	Page
Preserve large living trees, especially ones known for heavy flowering in winter	✓✓✓✓✓	10
Encourage the natural regeneration of trees and understorey trees and shrubs	✓✓✓✓	16
Preserve understorey trees and shrubs	✓✓✓	18
Rest areas of native vegetation from grazing	✓✓✓	16
Replant trees and understorey plants	✓✓	40

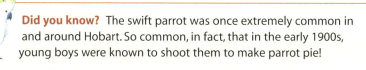

Did you know? The swift parrot was once extremely common in and around Hobart. So common, in fact, that in the early 1900s, young boys were known to shoot them to make parrot pie!

Glossy black-cockatoo
Calyptorhynchus lathamii

The glossy black-cockatoo is the smallest of the black-cockatoo group but it is still a relatively large (48 cm) black to brown-coloured cockatoo. The species has striking shiny black feathers on the wings and back, a scarlet-red panel in the tail which is barred with black feathers and edged with yellow in the female. Yellow neck patches on females are well developed in some populations.

Other common names: Casuarina cockatoo, casuarine, glossy cockatoo, Latham's cockatoo, Leach's black-cockatoo, Leach's red-tailed black-cockatoo, nutcracker.

Similar-looking species: Yellow-tailed black-cockatoo, red-tailed black-cockatoo.

Voice: A soft wailing 'kwee-chuck', 'tarr-red' or 'merrrve'.

Distribution: The glossy black-cockatoo has a patchy distribution that is strongly associated with she-oak trees. It occurs mainly in eucalypt open forests and woodlands including areas with cypress pine and brigalow. There are three sub-species—one is virtually confined to Kangaroo Island (although it is occasionally seen on the nearby mainland); a second occurs in the central-eastern Queensland; and a third

Esther Beaton

ranges from southern Queensland, through New South Wales to north-eastern Victoria.

Conservation status: The glossy black-cockatoo is declining in many parts of its range and the Kangaroo Island sub-species is classified as critically endangered. Habitat clearing for agriculture as well as the removal of large trees for firewood are the main processes threatening the survival of the species. Some populations are declining as a result of competition for hollows with introduced honey bees and other native hollow-users such as the common brushtail possum and the galah.

David Lindenmayer

Critical features of habitat: She-oak trees and large eucalypts with hollows

Key habitat needs: There are two key features of habitat for the glossy black-cockatoo: stands of she-oak trees that provide protein-rich food—it specialises in eating the seeds of a range of species of she-oaks—and large eucalypt trees with deep hollows where birds nest and raise their young.

What you can do on your land	Priority	Page
Preserve large living and dead trees, especially ones with hollows	✓✓✓✓✓	10
Preserve understorey trees and shrubs, particularly she-oaks	✓✓✓✓	18
Preserve native vegetation near creeks, wetlands and farm dams	✓✓✓	28
Encourage the natural regeneration of trees and understorey trees and shrubs	✓✓✓	16
Rest areas of native vegetation from grazing	✓✓✓	16
Replant trees and understorey plants, particularly local species of *Allocasuarina* and *Casuarina*	✓✓	40
Install nest boxes (using a design specifically tailored for the glossy black-cockatoo)	✓	12
Prevent illegal trapping on your land	✓	43

Did you know? Just as humans are either right or left-handed, many species of parrots are either right or left-footed. Studies of the glossy black-cockatoo show that the majority of birds are left-footed. For example, birds will use their bill to remove a she-oak cone and then hold it with their left foot to extract the seeds.

Sacred kingfisher
Todiramphus sanctus

The sacred kingfisher is a medium-sized (19–23.5 cm) kookaburra-like bird with dusty-turquoise-green head, black stripe through the eye, white collar, green back and buff-white underparts. The external characteristics of males and females are broadly similar.

Other common names: Green kingfisher, tree kingfisher, wood kingfisher.

Similar-looking species: Rainbow bee-eater, azure kingfisher.

Voice: Distinctive 'kek, kek, kek, kek' call. This is often repeated for prolonged periods throughout the day when birds first arrive back in their breeding territories.

Distribution: The sacred kingfisher is widespread across Australia in open forests, woodlands, rangelands, mallee and even mangroves, particularly along creek lines. It is absent from inland Australia except along creek lines. The species can be particularly abundant in some habitats like stands of river red gum forest. The sacred kingfisher is a summer migrant in south-eastern Australia (see the 'Did you know?' box opposite).

Esther Beaton

Conservation status: The sacred kingfisher is widespread and common.

Key habitat needs: The sacred kingfisher nests in tree hollows in many parts of its range. Therefore large trees that provide nesting cavities are a critical part of the habitat of the species. The species also can excavate a nesting burrow in termite nests and sometimes in river banks and roadside cuttings.

Trees

Mason Crane

Critical features of habitat: Tree hollows

What you can do on your land

	Priority	Page
Preserve large living and dead trees, especially ones with hollows	✓✓✓✓✓	10
Preserve native vegetation near creeks, wetlands and farm dams	✓✓✓✓	28
Preserve understorey trees and shrubs	✓✓✓	18
Encourage the natural regeneration of trees and understorey trees and shrubs	✓✓✓	16
Rest areas of native vegetation from grazing	✓✓✓	16
Replant trees and understorey plants	✓	40

Did you know? Many of Australia's birds are not all-year residents but move elsewhere in Australia or even to other countries and the Northern Hemisphere during certain seasons. The sacred kingfisher and the rufous whistler (on page 66) are examples of 'latitudinal migrants'—birds that breed in southern Australia during the spring and summer then travel northward in autumn to warmer environments such as those in northern New South Wales, Queensland, New Guinea and the islands to the north of the Australian continent. Another group of birds are 'altitudinal migrants' such as the scarlet robin (see page 68) that move to lower (warmer) elevations during the cooler winter months of the year.

Lace monitor
Varanus varius

The lace monitor is a large robust lizard growing to a maximum of 2 m but averaging 1.5 m from snout to tail. The species is dark blue/black with numerous white or yellow scales forming blotches or bands along the body. A light yellow and dark coloured broad-banded form also occurs in south-eastern Australia. The lace monitor is often active during the day capturing prey such as mammals, nestling birds, small lizards, and insects. The species also eats carrion such as road-killed mammals and birds. The lace monitor is mostly tree-dwelling, although it will venture to the ground in search of food. When alarmed, the lace monitor will readily climb the nearest tree or disappear into a hollow. One way of determining if there is a local population of the lace monitor is to inspect the trunks of smooth-barked eucalypts (like river red gum) for claw markings. Any tree used regularly will have abundant claw scars on the trunk.

Esther Beaton

Other common names: Tree goanna, goanna.

Similar-looking species: Heath monitor, sand monitor.

Distribution: The lace monitor is widely distributed throughout eastern Australia from south-eastern South Australia, through Victoria, New South Wales and as far north as Cape York Peninsula in northern Queensland.

Conservation status: The conservation status of the lace monitor in Victoria and the south-west slopes of New South Wales is uncertain, although the animal appears to be widely distributed but uncommon. The lace monitor has declined in many parts of its range due to land clearing, a deterioration in habitat quality (such as the loss of tree hollows), predation by feral predators, increased incidence of road kills, and illegal collecting.

Key habitat needs: The lace monitor is most commonly found in large areas of suitable woodland (> 50 ha in size) that support fallen hollow logs, trees with hollows, and termite mounds for depositing its eggs. The species is often encountered along roadside verges that are heavily timbered and occasionally seen scavenging around picnic spots and camp sites.

Damian Michael

Critical features of habitat: Large patches of remnant vegetation with tree hollows and fallen timber

What you can do on your land

	Priority	Page
Preserve large living and dead trees, especially ones with hollows	✓✓✓✓✓	10
Preserve understorey trees and shrubs	✓✓✓✓	18
Preserve ground cover of logs, leaf litter and ground vegetation cover	✓✓✓✓	22
Preserve native vegetation near creeks, wetlands and farm dams	✓✓✓	28
Encourage the natural regeneration of trees, understorey trees and shrubs	✓✓✓	16
Rest areas of native vegetation from grazing	✓✓✓	16
Control feral predators (and domestic cats)	✓✓✓	41
Replant trees and understorey plants	✓✓	40
Take care with hazard reduction burning, limit to paddock boundaries	✓✓	37
Prevent illegal trapping and hunting on your land	✓✓	43
Take care with the construction of roads and tracks	✓	43
Remove dead animals from roads to reduce lace monitor deaths from collisions with vehicles	✓	43

Did you know? The lace monitor belongs to a widespread group of 30 species of lizards that occur not only in Australia, but also in Asia and Africa. One of the members of the group is the giant komodo dragon (*Varanus komodoensis*) from Indonesia which can reach 3 m in length and which can prey on animals as large as a domestic goat. The number of Australian species in the group which contains the lace monitor is likely be an underestimate because reptiles have been poorly studied in comparison to other higher profile vertebrate groups such as birds and mammals. As an example, 386 new species of reptiles have been described since 1975—a staggering average of 15 per year!

Carpet python

Morelia spilota

(with various subspecies: *cheynei, imbricata, metcalfei, mcdowelli, spilota, variegata*)

variegata
cheynei
mcdowelli
spilota
metcalfei
imbricata

Esther Beaton

The carpet python is a large, non-venomous, thickset snake averaging 2 m in length, but sometimes reaching an impressive 4 m. The Murray/Darling form of the species is often a reddish-brown to tan colour with dorsally paired grey blotches or bands edged with black. An eastern form of the carpet python which also occurs within south-eastern Australia varies from light to dark brown with numerous irregular cream blotches edged with black and is larger than the Murray/Darling form.

Other common names: Carpet snake, diamond python.

Similar-looking species: None (although the venomous broad-headed snake is sometimes confused with the subspecies of diamond python around the Sydney region).

Distribution: The carpet python is widespread throughout many parts of northern, eastern and south-western Australia. The subspecies featured in this book occurs in South Australia, Victoria and inland New South Wales (another two subspecies are known from coastal New South Wales).

Conservation status: In Victoria, the carpet python is considered vulnerable to extinction due to its limited

distribution, and the patchy and isolated nature of many of the remaining populations. The species is uncommon on the south-western slopes of southern NSW, although it still occurs in areas containing suitable remnant vegetation. The carpet python is believed to have been introduced from other parts of Australia to control pest rodents in some parts of the southern slopes of New South Wales such as near the Murrumbidgee River (between Jugiong and Gundagai) and other areas along the Murray River.

Key habitat needs: The carpet python inhabits heavily timbered country with abundant large hollow-bearing trees and/or isolated rocky outcrops. A well-developed litter layer can also be important for the species providing camouflage to assist it in capturing prey.

The carpet python is sometimes encountered in the roofs and sheds of rural areas. It is a predominantly tree-dwelling animal that is active mostly at night or on warm evenings, utilising hollow logs, tree hollows, rabbit burrows, rock slabs and crevices for shelter during the day. The carpet python is sometimes encountered basking on branches or rocks slabs in the mid-morning sun before retreating within a shelter. It eats a variety of animals such as rodents, possums, rabbits, birds and other reptiles.

Damian Michael

Critical features of habitat: Tree hollows and fallen timber

What you can do on your land	Priority	Page
Preserve large living and dead trees, especially ones with hollows	✓✓✓✓✓	10
Preserve ground cover of logs, leaf litter, rocky outcrops and vegetation	✓✓✓✓	22
Preserve understorey trees and shrubs	✓✓✓	18
Preserve native vegetation near creeks, wetlands and farm dams	✓✓✓	28
Encourage the natural regeneration of trees, understorey trees and shrubs	✓✓✓	16
Rest areas of native vegetation from grazing	✓✓✓	16
Control feral predators (and domestic cats)	✓✓✓	41
Replant trees and understorey plants	✓✓	40
Take care with hazard reduction burning, limit to paddock boundaries	✓✓	37
Take care with the construction of roads and tracks	✓✓	43
Prevent illegal trapping and hunting on your land	✓✓	43

Did you know? Pythons have developed many special strategies to tackle the battle of the bulge. The pythons and closely related boas include both Australia's and the world's largest snakes and they are capable of swallowing prey with a diameter larger than their own. The jaw can be dislocated to eat large animals that have been captured. The skin can be greatly stretched to help a snake carry a swallowed animal while it is being digested. Once a snake has gorged itself, many of the internal organs undergo extraordinary changes to deal with a massive meal. For example, the small intestine can be expanded by up to three times. It then shrinks again once the prey has been digested and all the nutrients have been absorbed.

Peron's tree frog
Litoria peronii

Peron's tree frog is a medium-sized tree frog (44–65 mm) with very well-developed discs or pads on the ends of its fingers and toes. As with many tree frog species, Peron's tree frog can change the colour of its skin and may vary from almost transparent, through grey to a striking orange-bronze. These various base colours on the back are flecked with emerald green spots and the groin, inner and outer thigh region display a mottled combination of bright yellow and black. Another key feature of this species is the cross-shape of the pupil, particularly when the frog has been exposed to light for some time.

Andrew Claridge

Other common names: None.

Similar-looking species: Tyler's tree frog.

Voice: The breeding call of Peron's tree frog is a long, drawn-out descending rattling cackle or 'laugh' of up to 50 explosive notes that can be heard between late spring and summer. The call is often made from vegetation such as eucalypt trees well above the ground.

Distribution: Peron's tree frog occurs in South Australia, northern Victoria, New South Wales and southern Queensland. The species uses a wide array of habitats ranging from coastal forest and wetland and riparian habitats throughout to areas in and around rivers in drier inland regions.

Conservation status: Peron's tree frog is common and widespread.

Key habitat needs: Peron's tree frog is more likely to use farm dams if there is surrounding tree cover, which provides vertical habitat. It uses billabongs, wetlands and large pools within rivers that are surrounded by trees. The species can often be found under the loose bark of eucalypts. Males of the species often call from the edge of waterbodies particularly from areas with good vegetation cover.

Trees

Andrew Taylor Inset: Ken Griffiths

Critical features of habitat: Waterbodies surrounded by trees

What you can do on your land

	Priority	Page
Preserve large living and dead hollow trees, especially ones near waterbodies	✓✓✓✓✓	10
Avoid draining wetlands	✓✓✓✓✓	30
Preserve native vegetation near creeks, wetlands and farm dams	✓✓✓✓	28
Preserve understorey trees and shrubs	✓✓✓	18
Preserve ground cover of logs, leaf litter and ground vegetation cover	✓✓✓	22
Encourage the natural regeneration of trees and understorey trees and shrubs	✓✓✓	16
Rest areas of native vegetation from grazing	✓✓✓	16
Replant trees and understorey plants	✓✓	40
Take care with hazard reduction burning	✓✓	37
Control feral predators (and domestic cats)	✓✓	41

Did you know? Male frogs make all the noise and each species has a different call. The males are actually calling to attract a female so they can mate. Female frogs make sounds too, but they use their voice for other purposes, such as making distress calls that are designed to scare off predators that threaten to eat them.

Common ringtail possum

Pseudocheirus peregrinus

The common ringtail possum (60–70 cm) is a nocturnal possum weighing up to 1 kg. It has a long tapering prehensile tail (that is longer than the body) with a white tail tip with light brown (rufous-coloured) body fur. The fur colouring of the species can be highly variable throughout its distribution in eastern Australia. Both sexes are similar in appearance, although females have a pouch for suckling their young. At night, the presence of the common ringtail possum is sometimes given away by a high-pitched twittering call. The species spends almost all of its time foraging in trees and shrubs above the ground.

Other common names: South-eastern ringtail, rufous ringtail, Tasmanian ringtail, grey Queensland ringtail, banga.

Similar-looking species: Juveniles of the common brushtail possum.

Distribution: The common ringtail possum is widely distributed throughout eastern Australia from Cape York to Tasmania (including south-eastern South Australia). The species occupies a wide range of habitats including tea-tree swamps, open woodlands, dry and wet forests and rainforest. The common ringtail possum is also known from suburban gardens in larger cities such as Melbourne and Sydney.

Esther Beaton

Conservation status: The common ringtail possum is common and wide-spread, although it appears to have declined in some habitats such as those in the box-ironbark forests of north-eastern Victoria as a result of forestry operations, gold mining operations, land clearing, and the impacts of introduced predators such as the red fox and the feral cat.

Key habitat needs: Two key features appear to be important for the common ringtail possum—large old trees which are used for nesting and shelter sites and understorey vegetation such as tea-tree,

David Lindenmayer

Critical features of habitat: Understorey trees and shrubs and tree hollows

kunzea, and wattle. Tea-tree leaves are an important food source for the species in many parts of its distribution. The common ringtail possum will often build a stick nest (called a 'drey') in thickets of tea-tree and wattle, although in warm environments (woodland habitats) it prefers to use hollow trees for denning.

What you can do on your land	Priority	Page
Preserve large living and dead trees, especially ones with hollows	✓✓✓✓✓	10
Preserve understorey trees and shrubs	✓✓✓✓✓	18
Preserve native vegetation near creeks, wetlands and farm dams	✓✓✓✓	28
Encourage the natural regeneration of trees, understorey trees and shrubs	✓✓✓✓	16
Rest areas of native vegetation from grazing	✓✓✓	16
Control feral predators (and domestic cats)	✓✓✓	41
Replant trees and understorey plants	✓✓	40
Take care with hazard reduction burning, limit to paddock boundaries	✓✓	37

Did you know? The common ringtail possum produces two very different types of poo—one of which it eats. Hard dry faecal pellets or scats are excreted when animals are active at night and they fall to the ground. During the day when animals are resting in the nest, they produce a type of soft faeces which is low in fibre (that is difficult to digest) but high in key nutrients, particularly nitrogen. By eating soft faeces, the common ringtail possum can survive on a low nutrient diet of eucalypt leaves.

Rufous whistler
Pachycephala rufiventris

The presence of the rufous whistler (17 cm in size) is often revealed by its distinctive call (see below) with males doing most of the calling. The male has a white throat bordered by a thick black band, a grey back and rufous underparts. The female has brownish streaks on the throat and chest and is brownish-grey and olive on the back and flanks. The rufous whistler usually forages on branches and tree trunks.

Other common names: Rufous-breasted whistler, rufous-breasted thickhead, echong, mock whipbird, thunderbird.

Similar-looking species: Golden whistler, grey shrike-thrush.

Voice: Whipcrack 'ee-chong-chit' followed by 'joey-joey-joey'. This distinctive song is often repeated many times.

Distribution: The rufous whistler is distributed widely throughout mainland Australia in many types of vegetation including tall forests, open forest, woodland and shrubland (e.g. mallee and mulga).

Conservation status: The rufous whistler is common and widespread but is declining in those parts of its distribution where extensive land clearing has occurred.

Jean Paul Ferrero/Auscape

Key habitat needs: The rufous whistler will occur in many areas of native or exotic vegetation where there is a mixture of understorey and overstorey trees in which to forage.

Christopher MacGregor

Critical features of habitat: Shrubby understorey vegetation

What you can do on your land

	Priority	Page
Preserve large living and dead trees	✓✓✓✓	10
Preserve understorey trees and shrubs	✓✓✓✓	18
Preserve native vegetation near creeks, wetlands and farm dams	✓✓✓	28
Encourage the natural regeneration of trees, understorey trees and shrubs	✓✓✓	16
Rest areas of native vegetation from grazing	✓✓✓	16
Replant trees and understorey plants	✓✓	40
Take care with hazard reduction burning, limit to paddock boundaries	✓✓	37
Control feral predators (and domestic cats)	✓	41

Did you know? Like most species of birds, it is the male rufous whistler which is the most brightly coloured and also responsible for most of the calls. Calling takes energy and the amount of calling done by a male shows his quality or fitness to a potential female mate. If a territory maintained by a male has a good supply of food, then he can dedicate more time to calling. This tells females that he 'owns' a good quality territory that would be a good place for her to 'settle down' and have young.

Scarlet robin
Petroica multicolor

C. Andrew Henley/Auscape

Males and females of the scarlet robin (13 cm in size) are very different. The male has a brilliant scarlet breast, black throat and upperparts including wing flights. The wings have a bar of white and there is a distinctive white patch on the forehead. The female has a pale orange wash on the breast, grey-brown on her head and back, and a whitish forehead patch. The white-head patch on both sexes helps to distinguish the scarlet robin from other types of 'red robins'. The species has a distinctive foraging method—it perches on posts, stumps or low branches before it pounces on insect prey on the ground.

Other common names: Scarlet-breasted robin, white-capped robin.

Similar-looking species: Rose robin, flame robin, red-capped robin.

Voice: Descending 'seer-seer-seer' or 'wee-cheedalee-dalee'.

Distribution: The scarlet robin occurs throughout south-eastern Australia from Tasmania and southern South Australia to south-eastern Queensland. The species is also found in the south-west of Western Australia. The scarlet robin inhabits open forests and woodlands, as well as golf courses and parks. The species is an altitudinal migrant and in late autumn/winter it moves to warmer lower elevation areas, often in more open habitats.

Conservation status: Although the scarlet robin is widespread in south-eastern Australia, it is declining and becoming rare in southern South Australia and also in south-western Western Australia, largely due to land clearing with the destruction and deterioration of suitable habitat.

Key habitat needs: Scrubby understorey vegetation with a sparse layer of saplings and shrubs appears to be important for the scarlet robin—these provide places where they can forage and construct their nests.

Mason Crane

Critical features of habitat: Shrubby understorey vegetation

What you can do on your land

	Priority	Page
Preserve understorey trees and shrubs	✓✓✓✓✓	18
Preserve ground cover of logs, leaf litter and ground vegetation cover	✓✓✓✓	22
Preserve large living and dead trees	✓✓✓	10
Encourage the natural regeneration of trees, understorey trees and shrubs	✓✓✓	16
Rest areas of native vegetation from grazing	✓✓✓	16
Replant trees and understorey plants	✓✓	40
Control feral predators (and domestic cats)	✓✓	41

Did you know? The robins that occur in Australia are not even closely related to the robins from North America and Europe. Indeed, the scarlet robin is a member of a large group of birds comprised of 30 different species that are restricted to Australasia and Oceania. When European settlers first arrived in Australia they used the common names of familiar birds from their homeland. This is similar to the case of the magpie in Australia—a species that is also not related to its Northern Hemisphere namesake.

Yellow-footed antechinus
Antechinus flavipes

The yellow-footed antechinus is a small (16–32 cm) native marsupial with males weighing 25–80 g and females 20–50 g. The fur is slate-grey in colour on the head and brown-orange on the flanks, belly and feet. The tail tip is black. There is usually a ring of pale-coloured fur around the eye. Both sexes are similar in appearance although males are larger and females have a distinct area of naked skin on the belly with teats for suckling their young. The yellow-footed antechinus is sometimes seen during the day, particularly when it is overcast.

Other common names: Yellow-footed marsupial mouse, mardo (Western Australia).

Similar-looking species: Brown antechinus, agile antechinus, various species of dunnarts.

Distribution: The distribution of the yellow-footed antechinus encompasses south-east of South Australia through to northern Queensland (it is absent from Tasmania). The species also occurs in south-western Western Australia. The yellow-footed antechinus occupies a wide range of vegetation types from rainforest, swamps, dry forests and woodlands, and mulga.

Esther Beaton

Conservation status: The yellow-footed antechinus is widespread and common in some parts of its range.

Key habitat needs: The yellow-footed antechinus constructs nests in hollow trees and sometimes in fallen hollow logs. The species also forages in and around fallen timber. Understorey plants that provide nectar also can be important for this species.

Christopher MacGregor

Critical features of habitat: Large logs and fallen timber

What you can do on your land	Priority	Page
Preserve large living and dead trees, especially ones with hollows	✓✓✓✓✓	10
Preserve ground cover of logs, leaf litter and ground vegetation cover	✓✓✓✓✓	22
Preserve understorey trees and shrubs	✓✓✓✓	18
Control feral predators (and domestic cats)	✓✓✓✓	41
Preserve native vegetation near creeks, wetlands and farm dams	✓✓✓	28
Encourage the natural regeneration of trees, understorey trees and shrubs	✓✓✓	16
Rest areas of native vegetation from grazing	✓✓✓	16
Replant trees and understorey plants	✓✓	40
Take care with hazard reduction burning, limit to paddock boundaries	✓✓	37

Did you know? Like all the species of antechinus in Australia (there are at least eight and perhaps others yet to be described by scientists), all the adult males of the yellow-footed antechinus die late in the winter of each year. These animals have a two-week, 12 hour-a-day, mating frenzy before changes in hormone levels and deficiencies in the immune system contribute to their death.

Echidna

Tachyglossus aculeatus

The echidna cannot be confused with any other Australian mammal; the back and flanks are covered in straw-coloured spines and the head has a long tubular toothless snout. Both sexes are similar in appearance and it ranges from 33 to 45 cm in size. One of the best indicators of the presence of the echidna are semi-circular digs in the soil that are made in search of ants and termites.

Other common names: Short-beaked echidna, spiny anteater, porcupine.

Similar-looking species: None.

Distribution: The echidna is one of the most widespread Australian mammals, occurring throughout all of mainland Australia and also in Tasmania. The species inhabits an enormous range of forests, woodlands, rangelands, deserts, as well as other habitats.

Conservation status: The echidna is common and widespread.

Key habitat needs: The echidna is often found in areas with numerous logs and other fallen timber where they can forage and find shelter. Rock crevices and boulder piles are sometimes also used as shelter sites.

Esther Beaton

Mason Crane

Christopher MacGregor

Critical features of habitat: Large logs and fallen timber

What you can do on your land

	Priority	Page
Preserve ground cover of logs, leaf litter and ground vegetation cover	✓✓✓✓✓	22
Preserve large living and dead trees	✓✓✓✓	10
Preserve understorey trees and shrubs	✓✓✓	18
Avoid dismantling areas of surface rock	✓✓✓	25
Encourage the natural regeneration of trees, understorey trees and shrubs	✓✓✓	16
Rest areas of native vegetation from grazing	✓✓✓	16
Replant trees and understorey plants	✓✓	40
Take care with hazard reduction burning, limit to paddock boundaries	✓✓	37
Control feral predators (and domestic cats)	✓✓	41

Did you know? The echidna will take a bath when it's hot. This is because many of its activities are strongly influenced by temperature. When temperatures are hot, echidnas have been known to cool down in streams and ponds. They will also avoid extremely high daytime temperatures by being active at night.

Brown treecreeper
Climacteris picumnus

The head and neck of the brown treecreeper is grey with the rest of the body dull brown in colour. It has pale streaks on the rest of the body with pale bars on its tail. The male and the female are broadly similar in distinguishing features (size 16–18 cm). The brown treecreeper usually forages by spiralling up a tree trunk (hence the other common name of 'woodpecker'). It also searches for food on fallen logs and on the ground.

Other common names: Black treecreeper, woodpecker.

Similar-looking species: White-throated treecreeper, red-browed treecreeper.

Voice: Strident 'spink-spink' call that is often repeated.

Distribution: The brown treecreeper occurs through eastern Australia from Victoria to Cape York in far north Queensland (including South Australia) (absent from Tasmania) and inhabits dry open-forests and woodlands.

Conservation status: The brown tree-creeper is widespread, but is declining in those parts of its range which have been extensively cleared for farming, particularly where remaining patches of suitable habitat patches are isolated and fallen timber has been removed.

Esther Beaton

Key habitat needs: The brown treecreeper is often strongly associated with logs and fallen trees on the ground, particularly when they occur within large patches of remnant vegetation on relatively flat ground. Fallen trees are used for foraging and also for social interactions between adults and fledged juveniles. The brown treecreeper is also a hollow-user and builds a nest in hollow limbs or hollowed-out tree trunks. The connection of woodland areas appears to be important for the brown treecreeper as patches of remnant vegetation that are close to other sizeable areas of suitable woodland habitat are more likely to be occupied.

David Lindenmayer

Critical features of habitat: Large logs, fallen timber and tree hollows

What you can do on your land

	Priority	Page
Preserve large living and dead trees, especially ones with hollows	✓✓✓✓✓	10
Preserve ground cover of logs, leaf litter and ground vegetation cover	✓✓✓✓✓	22
Preserve understorey trees and shrubs	✓✓✓	18
Create artificial habitats with timber offcuts or discarded fence posts	✓✓✓	27
Preserve native vegetation near creeks, wetlands and farm dams	✓✓✓	28
Encourage the natural regeneration of trees, understorey trees and shrubs	✓✓✓	16
Rest areas of native vegetation from grazing	✓✓✓	16
Replant trees and understorey plants	✓✓	40
Control feral predators (and domestic cats)	✓✓	41
Take care with hazard reduction burning, limit to paddock boundaries	✓	37

Did you know? Brown treecreepers can be feisty animals engaging in tribal warfare. Territories are often occupied by a male and several helpers all of whom will help feed a breeding female. Coalitions of males may band together to drive out a male and his helpers in the adjacent territory. Such 'tribal warfare' involves a lot of calling, chest puffing, tail flicking and aggressive chases. Occasionally, opponents will grasp hold of one another—sometimes locking feet.

Bush stone-curlew
Burhinus grallarius

Andrew Claridge

The bush stone-curlew is a tall (50–60 cm) long-legged bird with a large 'staring' yellow eye and buff-white forehead. It has grey streaked upper parts. Males and females are broadly similar.

Other common names: Bush thick-knee, southern stone-curlew, weeloo, willaroo, bush curlew, land curlew, stone plover, high-legged plover, bridled plover.

Similar-looking species: Beach stone-curlew.

Voice: Eerie wailing 'wee-loo', 'wee-loo' call made at night and repeated with calls rising.

Distribution: The bush stone-curlew once occurred throughout much of mainland Australia, although it is absent from some drier inland arid areas without trees. The species is often associated with open grassy woodlands and rangelands (but not dense forest) and areas supporting native grasses.

Conservation status: Although the bush stone-curlew is common in northern Australia it is rare in southern Australia although it was once common. The species has been lost entirely from parts of its former range such as the Armidale Plateau in northern New South Wales as well as substantial areas of Victoria.

Numbers in southern Australia have been considerably reduced through land clearing, habitat deterioration, predation by feral predators and illegal hunting. The nests of the bush stone-curlew also appear to be vulnerable to trampling by domestic stock.

Key habitat needs: The bush stone-curlew appears to be strongly associated with logs, fallen trees and branches and coarse litter on the ground as well as cover of scattered shrubs.

Damian Michael

Critical features of habitat: Fallen timber and coarse leaf litter

What you can do on your land

	Priority	Page
Control feral predators (and domestic cats)	✓✓✓✓✓	41
Preserve ground cover of logs, leaf litter and ground vegetation cover	✓✓✓✓✓	22
Preserve areas of native grassland	✓✓✓✓✓	25
Preserve understorey trees and shrubs	✓✓✓✓	18
Encourage the natural regeneration of trees, understorey trees and shrubs	✓✓✓✓	16
Rest areas of native vegetation from grazing	✓✓✓✓	16
Preserve large living and dead trees	✓✓✓	10
Take care with hazard reduction burning	✓✓✓	37

Did you know? Birds sometimes imprint on humans as well as strange objects. An extraordinary case has been reported of a bush stone-curlew which 'bonded' with a motorbike. The particular individual slept near the wheel of the motorbike and then flew alongside it during outings! The 'partnership' ended when the bush stone-curlew paired up with another of its kind—leaving behind a heartbroken motorcycle.

Diamond firetail
Stagonopleura guttata

The diamond firetail is a small (12 cm) sparrow-like bird with striking red bill, a grey head and black flanks with brilliant white-spots. It has a bright red rump. The male and female are similar in appearance.

Other common names: Diamond finch, diamond sparrow, spotted-sided finch.

Similar-looking species: Red-browed firetail.

Voice: Mournful rising whistled 'tioo-wheee'.

Distribution: The diamond firetail occurs throughout eastern Australia from central Queensland to south-east South Australia (it is absent from Tasmania). The species inhabits a range of vegetation types from open eucalypt and cypress pine forests and woodlands, mallee and wattle scrubs.

Conservation status: The diamond firetail is now uncommon with populations believed to be in steep decline in Queensland, New South Wales, Victoria and South Australia, largely due to the clearing of woodland habitats and possibly also the invasion of exotic grasses that are not palatable for the species.

Stephen David Miller/Auscape

Key habitat needs: The diamond firetail is typically found in open forests, woodlands and mallee-dominated vegetation with a ground cover dominated by native grasses which provide a seed source.

Logs, rocks and ground cover

Mason Crane

Critical features of habitat:
Native grassland cover

What you can do on your land

	Priority	Page
Preserve areas of native grassland	✓✓✓✓✓	25
Rest areas of native vegetation from grazing	✓✓✓✓	16
Encourage the natural regeneration of trees, understorey trees and shrubs	✓✓✓	16
Take care with hazard reduction burning	✓✓✓	37
Preserve understorey trees and shrubs	✓✓✓	18
Preserve ground cover of logs, leaf litter and vegetation	✓✓✓	22
Replant trees and understorey plants	✓✓	40
Control feral predators (and domestic cats)	✓✓	41
Prevent illegal trapping and hunting on your land	✓✓	43

Did you know? The diamond firetail is a member of the finch family of birds. The finch group includes almost 20 species native to Australia—as well as one introduced species. Native species of finches became favoured birds for keeping in aviaries in Australia within a few years of European settlement. Australian finches are now kept in aviaries all over the world. Indeed, illegal poaching of wild populations of the diamond firetail for the cagebird industry may have contributed to the species' decline.

Olive legless lizard
Delma inornata

The olive legless lizard is a slender elongated ('snake-like') lizard that is light grey-brown to olive in colour often with a yellow tinge to its throat and side of its head. It reaches a maximum of 40 cm in length with the tail contributing to 75% of its body length. The species has conspicuous ear openings, a fleshy tongue, and vestigial hind leg flaps which distinguish it from juvenile venomous snakes. This species moves extremely quickly when disturbed, often performing one or two erratic jumps by springing from its coiled powerful tail. If handled roughly it will emit a short sharp squeak and sometimes shed its tail. It is mostly a nocturnal and crepuscular (active at dawn and dusk) species in warm weather, although it is occasionally active beneath shelter during the middle of the day.

Other common names: Unpatterned legless lizard.

Similar-looking species: Striped legless lizard, juvenile brown snake (but see the 'Did you know?' box opposite).

Distribution: The olive legless lizard occurs widely throughout eastern South Australia, Victoria, New South Wales and south-eastern Queensland. It inhabits areas inland of the Great Dividing Range.

Esther Beaton

Conservation status: The olive legless lizard is uncommon in Victoria and southern New South Wales and is patchily distributed. In areas supporting high quality grassland and/or grassy woodland habitats, it can be locally common. The conservation of the species is of concern because many areas of native grassland and grassy woodland have been replaced by paddocks dominated by annual pasture grasses and introduced plants which are unsuitable habitat.

Key habitat needs: The olive legless lizard is found in grasslands and grassy woodlands on the slopes and flats. It is often encountered during the day under small rocks embedded in the ground or among fallen timber. The species also uses the base of grass tussocks (including phalaris) and invertebrate burrows for shelter and foraging.

Christopher MacGregor

Critical features of habitat: Intact native grassland and grassy woodland

What you can do on your land	Priority	Page
Preserve areas of native grassland	✓✓✓✓✓	25
Try to leave some unploughed areas	✓✓✓✓✓	26
Preserve ground cover of logs, leaf litter and ground vegetation cover	✓✓✓✓	22
Preserve understorey trees and shrubs	✓✓✓	18
Take care with hazard reduction burning, limit to paddock boundaries	✓✓✓	37
Control feral predators (and domestic cats)	✓✓✓	41
Rest areas of native vegetation from grazing	✓✓	16
Replant trees and understorey plants	✓	40

Did you know? The olive legless lizard belongs to a unique group of lizards that are virtually confined to Australia (33 species) and New Guinea (2 species). Unfortunately, despite its status as a 'true-blue Aussie', the olive legless lizard is often killed because of its superficial resemblance to the juvenile (and highly venomous) brown snake. However, there are several straightforward ways to quickly identify the olive legless lizard. First, the olive legless lizard has prominent ear openings which never occur in the brown snake. Second, the olive legless lizard (and most other closely related species of legless lizards in south-eastern Australia) have no dark markings on the head. Juvenile brown snakes also have black bands spanning the head, neck and sometimes the entire body. Third, the olive legless lizard often squeaks when alarmed—something which the brown snake never does. Fourth, the olive legless lizard has a fleshy tongue (similar to that of geckos—to which legless lizards are very closely related). The brown snake has a forked tongue.

Southern rainbow skink
Carlia tetradactyla

The southern rainbow skink is a small robust lizard reaching a maximum of 15 cm from head to tail with a rich brown back with darker and lighter flecks merging to form a single central and lateral stripe. It is distinguished by having four fingers and five toes, the only lizard of its size in south-eastern Australia to have this combination. Breeding males often display a bright flush of aqua-blue and orange beneath the throat and along their flanks. The southern rainbow skink can be found underneath fallen timber/rocks and is often seen among leaf litter around the base of large trees. It is a diurnal lizard, which catches small insects and termites during the day.

Other common names: Four-fingered skink.

Similar-looking species: Several other species of small skinks.

Distribution: The southern rainbow skink is distributed from northern Victoria through New South Wales and south-eastern Queensland.

Conservation status: The southern rainbow skink is uncommon in Victoria and on the southern slopes of New South Wales and is known to have a patchy distribution. The species may be declining, most likely because of the removal of fallen timber, woody debris and leaf litter from remnant woodlands and around paddock trees.

Key habitat needs: The southern rainbow skink is found in dry forests, open woodland and grassy ecosystems that support abundant fallen timber, woody debris, leaf litter and tussock grasses.

David Lindenmayer

Critical features of habitat: Fallen timber and abundant leaf litter

What you can do on your land

	Priority	Page
Preserve ground cover of logs, leaf litter and ground vegetation cover	✓✓✓✓✓	22
Preserve large living and dead trees	✓✓✓	10
Preserve understorey trees and shrubs	✓✓✓	18
Encourage the natural regeneration of trees, understorey trees and shrubs	✓✓✓	16
Rest areas of native vegetation from grazing	✓✓✓	16
Control feral predators (and domestic cats)	✓✓✓	41
Take care with hazard reduction burning, limit to paddock boundaries	✓✓✓	37
Replant trees and understorey plants	✓	40

Did you know? The southern rainbow skink, like many species of lizards, will shed its tail when being handled. This is a strategy to help it escape from predators as the wriggling tail can be cast off while the rest of the lizard scurries away. However, in the case of male lizards, the presence of a tail is a sign of its social status and careful research has shown that lizards without tails are far less likely to reproduce.

Marbled gecko
Christinus marmoratus

The marbled gecko varies markedly in colouration between locations and seasons from light grey to brown with a dark reticulated pattern encompassing its entire dorsal surface. The species reaches a maximum length of just over 10 cm from snout to tail, although animals smaller than this are common. The tail can constitute 50% of the body length, although the marbled gecko is often found with incomplete or partly regenerating tails of a different colour. The marbled gecko is nocturnal and actively forages above the ground for insects. Animals have been observed catching insects that have been attracted to household lights on warm evenings. When handled, the marbled gecko (like many other species of small lizards) will shed its tail which can then take many months to regenerate.

Esther Beaton

Other common names: Southern marbled gecko.

Similar-looking species: Several other species of geckos (particularly the tree dtella and eastern spiny-tailed gecko).

Distribution: The marbled gecko has a southern Australian distribution occurring in wetter types of habitats from south-western Western Australia, southern South Australia, Victoria and southern and central New South Wales.

Conservation status: The marbled gecko is common in Victoria and southern New South Wales, although its distribution is often patchy and localised.

Key habitat needs: The marbled gecko has adapted to the cool dry forests and woodlands of south-eastern Australia. Within the south-west slopes of south-eastern Australia, the species is commonly encountered beneath the strips of bark on large mature eucalypts such as river red gum and yellow box. It also occurs under rock slabs, especially those lying on other rocks, and beneath fallen timber.

David Lindenmayer

Critical features of habitat:
Large living and dead trees
and fallen timber

What you can do on your land

What you can do on your land	Priority	Page
Preserve ground cover of logs, leaf litter and ground vegetation cover	✓✓✓✓✓	22
Preserve large living and dead trees, especially ones that shed large amounts of bark	✓✓✓✓	10
Encourage the natural regeneration of trees, understorey trees and shrubs	✓✓✓	16
Rest areas of native vegetation from grazing	✓✓✓	16
Take care with hazard reduction burning, limit to paddock boundaries	✓✓	37
Control feral predators (and domestic cats)	✓✓	41
Preserve understorey trees and shrubs	✓✓	18
Replant trees and understorey plants	✓	40

Did you know? Geckos have some remarkable lifestyle adaptations. One such adaptation is spatula-like toe pads that allow them to climb on even the most slippery of surfaces such as vertical panes of glass. Another is a long tongue which is often used to clean the surface of the eye—an essential function since geckos do not have eyelids.

Cunningham's skink
Egernia cunninghami

Cunningham's skink is a large, robustly built, brown, rough-skinned lizard reaching a maximum length of 40 cm often with dark and light blotches or flecks marbling the body. The species has a body covered in large keeled scales and a stout spiny tail. Cunningham's skink is often encountered during the day in small to large groups basking on granite rock outcrops. If disturbed, the species will readily disappear within a crevice jamming its body and tail against the sides to prevent it being dislodged.

Other common names: None.

Similar-looking species: Rock skink, tree skink.

Distribution: Cunningham's skink occurs from western Victoria through eastern New South Wales to south-eastern Queensland. There are also isolated populations of the species in the Mount Lofty Ranges near Adelaide in South Australia.

Conservation status: Cunningham's skink is uncommon in Victoria and the southern slopes of New South Wales and it has a patchy and localised distribution. Many granite outcrops are now isolated by cultivated and/or grazed paddocks and a reduction in

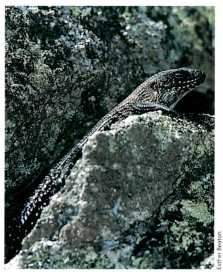

Esther Beaton

native vegetation (especially flowering herbs and shrubs and a shift towards annual pasture grasses and woody weeds) may have resulted in some local populations becoming extinct.

Key habitat needs: Cunningham's skink occurs in a wide variety of agricultural, woodland and forest habitats but is always closely associated with granite boulders and other rocky outcrops.

Damian Michael

Critical features of habitat: Granite outcrops

What you can do on your land

	Priority	Page
Limit grazing pressure among rocky outcrops	✓✓✓✓✓	25
Rest areas of native vegetation from grazing	✓✓✓✓	16
Preserve ground cover of logs, leaf litter and ground vegetation cover	✓✓✓	22
Take care with hazard reduction burning, limit to paddock boundaries	✓✓	37
Control feral predators (and domestic cats)	✓✓	41

Did you know? Male lizards (and snakes) have not one but two penises. The reasons they have developed such bizarre sexual apparatus are not known but one theory suggests that the ancient ancestors of lizards and snakes gave up having a penis. At a later stage, the ancestors of lizards and snakes then re-invented the reptile penis and the 'two-pronged' version evolved. Complex sexual organs occur because of what has been termed the 'lock and key hypothesis'. The male sexual organ (the penis) is the key which will only fit the right 'lock' (i.e. the female organs)— ensuring that sex can only occur between members of the same species. Different 'locks and keys' then develop when a new species evolves.

Green and golden bell frog
Litoria aurea

The green and golden bell frog is a large (57–108 mm) tree frog which is quite similar to several other, closely related species that occur within south-eastern Australia. Collectively these species are known as 'bell frogs' and the group also includes the southern bell frog. Bell frogs are distinctive in relation to their call, size, colouring and behaviour and are often described by landholders as large bright green and golden tree frogs that are readily seen during the day basking among aquatic vegetation. The green and golden bell frog has a background colour of green with irregular and quite variable patches of gold spots. It has quite large discs or pads on the ends of its fingers and toes and its skin is quite smooth. It has a white or yellow stripe that runs down the side of the head and continues as a fold of skin down the side of its body. This is underlined with a dark stripe. The groin and hindside of the thighs are distinctly blue. This species is often active during the day.

Other common names: None.

Similar-looking species: Southern bell frog.

Voice: The green and golden bell frog has a loud call that is slow and guttural in four parts: 'craw-awk, crawk, crok, crok'.

Esther Beaton

Distribution: Occurs in eastern and south-eastern New South Wales and far-eastern Victoria around permanent water bodies including streams, swamps, lagoons and farm dams.

Conservation status: The species was common until the early 1980s but has declined significantly since then and the species has disappeared from much of its former range. A fungal disease is a major suspected causal factor, although loss of habitat, introduced fish predators and altered ultraviolet radiation regimes are also thought to have contributed to demise of the species.

Key habitat needs: The species inhabits permanent water bodies, swamps, billabongs, farm dams and slow-flowing streams. It is limited in its ability to use vertical habitat such as trees and is unable to burrow. In addition, the large body size of the species precludes it from squeezing into small soil cracks and crevices suitable for small ground-dwelling frogs. During dry times, the species most likely relies on thick vegetation, rocks, logs and large soil cracks in moist environments to provide refuge. The green and golden bell frog is likely to have been negatively affected by the loss of ponds and soil moisture that has occurred through gully erosion. This form of land degradation is widespread across much of south-eastern Australia.

Donna Hazell

Critical features of habitat: Permanent waterbodies with thick surrounding ground cover vegetation

What you can do on your land

	Priority	Page
Preserve native vegetation near creeks, wetlands and farm dams	✓✓✓✓✓	28
Avoid draining wetlands	✓✓✓✓✓	30
Preserve large living and dead trees	✓✓✓✓	10
Preserve understorey trees and shrubs	✓✓✓	18
Preserve ground cover of logs, leaf litter and ground vegetation cover	✓✓✓	22
Avoid introducing mosquito fish to waterbodies	✓✓✓	33
Control direct stock access to dams	✓✓✓	31
Encourage the natural regeneration of trees, understorey trees and shrubs	✓✓✓	16
Rest areas of native vegetation from grazing	✓✓✓	16
Replant trees and understorey plants, focus efforts on the upstream section where the water flows in	✓✓	40
Control feral predators (and domestic cats)	✓✓	41

Did you know? Not all tree frogs can climb. Tree frogs belong to a family of frogs (called the Hylidae) that share skeletal characteristics of the pectoral girdle and the fingers and toes. Although many tree frogs are characterised by enlarged pads on their fingers and toes, this is not a feature of all species in the family. Some tree frogs spend most of their life on the ground, such as the whistling tree frog. The finger and toe pads of this species are barely visible.

Platypus

Ornithorhynchus anatinus

Weighing about 1.7 kg and 44–55 cm in length, no other animal has the extraordinary combination of features of the platypus—a duck-bill, webbed feet, and a rounded tail—features which led early scientists to believe that the species was a hoax! The platypus also has white fur around the eyes. In the water, the species can be confused with the water rat but it does not swim 'dog-paddle' like the water rat. Both sexes are similar in appearance, although males are larger and have a 1+ cm long spur on each hind foot.

Esther Beaton

Other common names: Duck-billed platypus.

Similar-looking species: None.

Distribution: The platypus is distributed along the east coast of Australia from far north Queensland to western Victoria (including Tasmania). It formerly occurred in South Australia, but wild populations now appear to be extinct there. The platypus is found in aquatic environments within a wide range of vegetation types including sub-alpine areas, eucalypt forests and woodland, and tropical rainforest.

Conservation status: The platypus is common and widespread, but regarded as vulnerable in many parts of its distribution due to altered streambank conditions (e.g. tree removal and bank erosion) as well as the declining quality and condition of aquatic environments.

Key habitat needs: The platypus appears to prefer streams and watercourses where the banks are steep (but stable) and soils are friable (to facilitate burrowing for nesting).

Creeks, wetlands and dams

Damian Michael

Critical features of habitat: Stable streambanks and undegraded waterways

What you can do on your land	Priority	Page
Preserve native vegetation near creeks and wetlands	✓✓✓✓✓	28
Avoid draining wetlands	✓✓✓✓✓	30
Rest areas of native vegetation from grazing	✓✓✓✓	16
Avoid removing snags (fallen logs) from rivers and watercourses	✓✓✓✓	28
Replant trees and understorey plants to stabilise streambanks	✓✓	40
Take care with the disposal of pesticides, herbicides and other chemicals, to prevent leakage into creeks, wetlands and farm dams	✓✓	33
Avoid fishing with gill nets and drum nets as they will drown animals	✓✓	–
Avoid constructing dams with deep, still water	✓	–

Did you know? Sixty-million-year-old fossil teeth of the platypus have been found in Patagonia in the far south of South America. The existence of the platypus in Australia and South America is strong evidence these continents were once part of the same land-mass called Gondwana (that also included New Zealand and Antarctica).

Common eastern froglet
Crinia signifera

The common eastern froglet is a small frog (18–28 mm) that is highly variable in colour, pattern and skin texture— sometimes making identification difficult. Colour may range from grey through to brown or black, although all individuals have black and white mottling on their underbelly. The male breeding call may be confused with crickets, particularly when individuals call during the day.

Other common names: Common froglet, clicking froglet.

Similar-looking species: Eastern sign-bearing frog.

Voice: The common eastern froglet is a ubiquitous species that is quite loud for its comparatively small size. It makes a 'crick.…crick….crick' call.

Distribution: The common eastern froglet occurs in south-eastern South Australia, Tasmania, Victoria, New South Wales and south-eastern Queensland. The species will occur in almost every habitat within the limits of its distribution.

Conservation status: The common eastern froglet is one of the most common and widespread species of frogs in south-eastern Australia.

Ken Griffiths

Key habitat needs: The common eastern froglet will breed at any time of the year in a wide range of environments, including streams, wetlands, farm dams, boggy areas and even roadside ditches with temporary standing water. On the farm, they may be seen hopping away during lawn-mowing in the home paddock, or found sheltering under logs or rocks in the garden, around farm dams or other water bodies. They also may occur under corrugated iron left on the ground.

Donna Hazell

Critical features of habitat: Any type of water body

What you can do on your land	Priority	Page
Preserve native vegetation near creeks, wetlands and farm dams	✓✓✓✓	28
Avoid draining wetlands	✓✓✓✓	30
Preserve ground cover of logs, leaf litter and ground vegetation cover	✓✓	22

Did you know? Not all frogs lay their eggs in water. Some species in south-eastern Australia lay their eggs in damp places on the land, hidden amongst thick vegetation or under rocks and logs. These species include the brown toadlet, and other closely related species in the *Pseudophryne* genus (e.g. Bibron's toadlet—see page 98) as well as the Baw Baw frog and the eastern smooth frog.

Spotted marsh frog
Limnodynastes tasmaniensis

The spotted marsh frog is a small to medium-sized frog (31–47 mm) which is grey-green to buff in colour with khaki green blotches on its back and broad stripes of the same colour on its arms and legs. Individuals often have a yellow or orange stripe down the middle of their back. After torrential rain when low lying areas become inundated, this species is often responsible for the numerous frothy egg masses that can be seen floating in the shallow water near emergent aquatic vegetation. The spotted marsh frog breeds between spring and early summer.

Other common names: Spotted grass frog.

Similar-looking species: Long-thumbed frog.

Voice: The call of the spotted marsh frog varies depending upon where individuals occur within its overall distribution. In south-eastern Australia the call is a sharp 'click' or a series of rapid clicks—'uk-uk-uk-uk-uk-uk'—that are not unlike the sound of a machine gun.

Distribution: The spotted marsh frog is widely distributed from south-eastern South Australia, Tasmania, New South Wales and Queensland. The spotted marsh frog occurs in a wide range of habitats from wet coastal forests to interior arid lands.

Conservation status: The spotted marsh frog is common and widespread.

Key habitat needs: The spotted marsh frog uses temporary water bodies, wetlands and farm dams. The species may occur under corrugated iron, fence posts and bricks left on the ground that act as moist refugia and provide protection from predators. Soil cracks are also important refuge sites. The species can produce large choruses around temporary wetlands or in areas alongside rivers that become

Donna Hazell

Critical features of habitat: Any type of water body with emergent vegetation

inundated after heavy rains or high flow events. Studies have shown that the spotted marsh frog is more likely to occur at water bodies with plenty of vegetation growing in the shallow water zone and lots of vegetation, such as grasses and sedges growing in the area immediately surrounding the water body. The species also appears to prefer water bodies that do not contain fish.

What you can do on your land	Priority	Page
Preserve native vegetation near creeks, wetlands and farm dams	✓✓✓✓✓	28
Avoid draining wetlands	✓✓✓✓	30
Avoid releasing fish into all farm dams on a property	✓✓✓	33

Did you know? There are frogs that sun-bake. Some frogs lose moisture through their skin at the same rate as free-standing water and remain hidden during the day to avoid dehydration. There are others, however, such as the green and golden bell frog and the southern bell frog that deliberately bask in the sun to warm themselves. Some species actually secrete substances that act as barriers against moisture loss.

Striped marsh frog
Limnodynastes peronii

The striped marsh frog is a medium-sized frog (48–73 mm) with stripes running the length of its body in dark and light brown and cream colours. These markings provide excellent camouflage in grass cover and leaf litter.

Other common names: Brown-striped frog.

Similar-looking species: Salmon-striped frog.

Voice: The striped marsh frog is a fairly secretive species that is often seen but not heard. Its call is a 'whuck' that resembles the sound of a tennis ball being hit with a racket. The call can be heard between spring and early summer.

Distribution: The striped marsh frog occurs throughout coastal eastern Australia from Tasmania to far north Queensland.

Conservation status: The striped marsh frog is common and widespread.

Esther Beaton

Key habitat needs: The striped marsh frog is a ground-dwelling frog that breeds in ponds and slow-flowing streams that are well vegetated, allowing individuals to call from hidden places. The species is very common in urban environments. It often does not occur around constructed water bodies like farm dams because of the lack of vegetation cover. As with many species of Australian frogs, there is virtually no information on where this species goes after the breeding season.

Donna Hazell

Critical features of habitat: Natural ponds, slow-flowing creeks and farm dams with good vegetation cover

What you can do on your land

	Priority	Page
Preserve large living and dead trees, particularly around waterbodies	✓✓✓✓✓	10
Preserve understorey trees and shrubs, particularly around waterbodies	✓✓✓✓✓	28
Preserve ground cover of logs, leaf litter and ground vegetation cover, particularly around waterbodies	✓✓✓✓	22
Avoid draining wetlands	✓✓✓✓	30
Encourage the natural regeneration of trees, understorey trees and shrubs	✓✓✓	16
Rest areas of native vegetation from grazing	✓✓✓	16
Replant trees and understorey plants	✓✓	40

Did you know? The females do the heavy lifting in the frog world. When it comes time to mate the female frog carries the male to a place that she thinks is suitable for laying her eggs. But first she has to transport the male from the place he has chosen as his calling site. This can mean quite a bit of work as some males can call many metres away from the nearest suitable place to lay eggs. It's a good thing that male frogs are generally smaller than females!

Bibron's toadlet
Pseudophryne bibronii

Bibron's toadlet is a small (22–32 mm) ground-dwelling frog that is quite secretive and difficult to find. The species breeds in autumn. It is quite dark in colour and is sometimes almost black. Its skin is quite warty and it has a distinctive bold pattern of black and white blotches or marbling on the underside. The outer thigh region has pale yellow or orange coloured markings and it also has buff markings immediately behind its arms.

Other common names: Brown toadlet.

Similar-looking species: Southern toadlet.

Voice: Short call of 'ark'.

Distribution: Bibron's toadlet is a widely distributed species from south-eastern South Australia, Tasmania, Victoria, New South Wales and central Queensland.

Conservation status: It appears that Bibron's toadlet has declined across south-eastern Australia and the species needs urgent research and conservation management attention to ensure that it does not disappear from agricultural areas.

Ken Griffiths

Andrew Claridge

Key habitat needs: Unlike most frog species that occur in the temperate zone, Bibron's toadlet lays its eggs on land, in moist well-vegetated places like seepages, sheltered moist gullies and swampy meadows. Their eggs are equipped with a substantial amount of yolk, allowing the tadpoles to develop to an advanced stage within the egg capsule. Bibron's toadlet relies on overland flow from rainfall events to flush the well-developed tadpoles into adjacent depressions that last long enough for the tadpoles to complete their development. The loss of wet, boggy environments, through gully erosion and soil compaction, is likely to have reduced the availability of habitat for this species in agricultural areas of south-eastern Australia.

Donna Hazell

Critical features of habitat: Well vegetated boggy areas

What you can do on your land	Priority	Page
Preserve ground cover of logs, leaf litter and ground vegetation cover	✓✓✓✓✓	22
Preserve native vegetation near creeks, wetlands and farm dams	✓✓✓✓✓	28
Avoid draining wetlands	✓✓✓✓✓	30
Rest areas of native vegetation from grazing, particularly wet and boggy areas	✓✓✓✓	32
Encourage the natural regeneration of trees, understorey trees and shrubs	✓✓✓	16
Control feral predators (and domestic cats)	✓✓✓	41
Replant trees and understorey plants	✓✓	40

Did you know? Most frogs have to close their eyes to swallow their food. Once a frog has caught its prey, it holds it in its mouth. A muscular retraction of the eyes means that they bulge down into the mouth cavity which helps push food down the animal's gullet.

Smooth toadlet
Uperoleia laevigata

The smooth toadlet is a small frog (20–32 mm) which is brown or olive in colour with blotches of khaki green or dark brown on the upper surface of its body. Almost all individuals have a triangular patch of pale colour between the eyes and down to the nose. There is a patch of red-orange in the groin and behind each knee. Individuals have enlarged glands on either side of the head just above and behind the eyes.

Other common names: Orange-groined toadlet.

Similar-looking species: Tyler's toadlet, dusky toadlet.

Ken Griffiths

Distribution: The smooth toadlet is distributed throughout eastern Australia from Victoria to south-east Queensland throughout a wide range of habitats from grassland to forest.

Voice: The smooth toadlet makes a long pulsed 'aaank' call exceeding more than half a second in length.

Conservation status: The smooth toadlet is common and widespread.

Key habitat needs: The smooth toadlet occurs in a wide range of vegetation types from grassland to forest. It breeds in wetlands, inundated grasslands, farm dams and other types of still water bodies. When the smooth toadlet is not active, it seeks shelter under logs, rocks and leaf litter.

Damian Michael

Critical features of habitat: Any water body with ground cover, leaf litter and fallen timber nearby

What you can do on your land

	Priority	Page
Preserve ground cover of logs, leaf litter and vegetation, particularly near waterbodies	✓✓✓✓✓	22
Preserve native vegetation near creeks, wetlands and farm dams	✓✓✓✓✓	28
Avoid draining wetlands	✓✓✓✓	30
Preserve large living and dead trees, particularly near waterbodies	✓✓✓	10
Preserve understorey trees and shrubs, particularly near waterbodies	✓✓✓	18
Encourage the natural regeneration of trees, understorey trees and shrubs	✓✓✓	16
Rest areas of native vegetation from grazing	✓✓✓	16
Take care with hazard reduction burning, limit to paddock boundaries	✓✓	37
Control feral predators (and domestic cats)	✓✓	41
Replant trees and understorey plants	✓	40

Did you know? There are no Aussie toads (except for the introduced cane toad), but there are several Australian frogs that look like toads. The banjo frog for example, is often labelled as a 'big ugly toad' when unexpectedly dug up in the vegetable patch. Common names of many frog species include words such as 'toadlet'. It's therefore not surprising that many people think there are native Australian toads.

Booroolong frog
Litoria booroolongensis

Ken Griffiths

The Booroolong frog is a medium sized frog (36–54 mm) that may vary in colour from grey, olive or reddish-brown with a net-like pattern of black markings and salmon-coloured flecks. A very thin black stripe runs from the nose through the eye over the top of the ear to the shoulder. Finger and toe pads are clearly visible, but not large. The toes are strongly webbed and the backs of the thighs are dark brown with pale spots. The Booroolong frog may be confused with the more common Lesueur's frog as they are similar in appearance and both inhabit stream environments. Lesueur's frog has less webbing on the toes, and a more distinct black line running from the nose to the shoulder.

Other common names: None.

Similar-looking species: Lesueur's frog.

Voice: This species has a very soft purring call of 'qrk-qrk-qrk' that may be heard during the spring breeding season (October through to December).

Distribution: The Booroolong frog occurs mainly in western-flowing streams of the Great Dividing Range from 200 to 1300 m above sea level in New South Wales and north-eastern Victoria.

Conservation status: The Booroolong Frog has declined from parts of New South Wales with recent surveys failing to locate the species in areas where it was formerly abundant. The species is only known from two localities in Victoria, both of which are highly degraded and exposed to a range of threats. Reasons for the decline of this species remain unclear with a range of possible causal factors. These include vegetation clearance, grazing, willow invasion, altered stream flow due to hydro-electric schemes and irrigation, introduced fish (trout), foxes and feral cats, climate change, herbicides, and disease.

Key habitat needs: The species inhabits permanent streams within a range of forest and woodland communities.

Dave Hunter

Critical features of habitat: Slow-flowing creeks and rivers with cobbled banks

It also uses streams in cleared grazing land. The Booroolong frog usually occurs on cobbled banks near slow-flowing creeks and rivers with ferns, grasses or sedges growing along the edge of the stream. Exposed rocks alongside the stream provide basking sites and calling sites for the males.

What you can do on your land	Priority	Page
Preserve native vegetation near creeks, wetlands and farm dams	✓✓✓✓✓	28
Minimise disturbance to cobbled sections of creeks	✓✓✓✓✓	31
Rest areas of native vegetation around streams from grazing	✓✓✓✓	30
Avoid draining wetlands	✓✓✓	30
Take care with hazard reduction burning, limit to paddock boundaries	✓✓	37
Replant trees and understorey plants	✓	40
Control feral predators (and domestic cats)	✓	41

Did you know? Frogs can be natural pest controllers. Frogs eat a wide range of insects and other small creatures that are best kept in low numbers in your garden and in the paddock. These include spiders, beetles and their larvae, flies, mites, earwigs, cockroaches, termites, grasshoppers, crickets, moths and butterflies, millipedes, bugs, ants and springtails.

Glossary

Algal blooms
an outbreak of algae or cyanobacteria as a result of excess nutrients in the water. These microorganisms can produce toxic compounds that can kill fish.

Arboreal
species that live in trees (tree-dwelling).

Cobbled
an area with numerous stones or small boulders; usually refers to a section of a streambank.

Crepuscular
active at dawn and dusk.

Critical weight range
a widely held belief that terrestrial species of intermediate (50 g to 5 kg) size are more prone to extinction risks than small or large species.

Defoliate
to strip of leaves.

Dieback
occurs when a tree is stressed either by living (e.g. insect defoliation) or non-living (e.g. drought) factors, which then renders it susceptible to secondary attack by disease, fungus or insects and perhaps leads to the death of the tree.

Diurnal
species that are active in the daytime.

Dorsal(ly)
refers to the top or back surface of the body.

Ecosystem
a community of different species interdependent on each other as well as with their non-living environment.

Emergent
a property of vegetation (vegetation that is higher than the surrounds such as trees emerging above the understorey or wetland plants emerging above the water surface).

Eutrophication
the enrichment of bodies of fresh water with nutrients such as nitrate and phosphate (due to fertiliser run-off, sewage, sediments) that can result in algal blooms and in some cases suppress the growth of aquatic plants and kill aquatic fauna.

Habitat
the range of environments in which a species can occur, survive and reproduce.

Invertebrate
an animal without a backbone (all animals other than fish, frogs, reptiles, birds and mammals).

Mycorrhizae
a mutually beneficial (or symbiotic) relationship between fungi and plants.

Nocturnal or crepuscular
animals that are most active around dusk and dawn.

Ornithologist
a person who studies birds.

Riparian vegetation
vegetation growing on the banks of streams or rivers.

Terrestrial
occurring on land.

Truffle
the fruiting body of a fungus that forms under the ground and which provides an important food resource for many species of mammals.

Vertebrate
an animal with a backbone (i.e. fish, frogs, reptiles, birds and mammals).

Vestigial
body parts or organs that are smaller, simpler and non-functional in their present condition but which were complete and functional in an ancestral species.

General reading

General

Anonymous (2001). *Paddock trees. Who'll miss them when they are gone?* Pamphlet produced by NSW National Parks and Wildlife Service, NSW Department of Land and Water Conservation, and Greening Australia.

Breckwoldt, R. (1983). *Wildlife in the home paddock: Nature conservation for Australian farmers.* Angus & Robertson, Melbourne.

Burgman, M.A. & Lindenmayer, D.B. (1998). *Conservation biology for the Australian environment.* Surrey Beatty and Sons, Chipping Norton.

Campbell, A. (1991). *Planning for sustainable farming: The Potter Farmland Plan story.* Lothian, Melbourne.

Department of Land and Water Conservation (1998). *The constructed wetlands manual.* New South Wales Department of Land and Water Conservation, Sydney.

Goldney, D. & Wakefield, S. (1997). *Save the bush toolkit.* Charles Sturt University, Bathurst.

Grant, J. (1997). *The nestbox book.* Gould League, Kew, Melbourne.

Woinarski, J.C., Recher, H.F. & Majer, J.D. (1997). Vertebrates of eucalypt formations. pp. 303–41. In *Eucalypt ecology. Individuals to ecosystems.* J. Williams & J. Woinarski, editors. Cambridge University Press, Melbourne.

Birds

Barrett, G. (2000). Birds on farms: Ecological management for agricultural sustainability. Supplement to *Wingspan*, **10(4)**. Birds Australia, Hawthorn, Victoria.

Garnett, S.T. & Crowley, G.M. (2000). *The Action Plan for Australian birds.* Natural Heritage Trust, Canberra.

Greening Australia. (2001). *Bringing birds back. A glovebox guide for bird identification and habitat restoration in ACT and SE NSW.* Greening Australia, ACT and SE NSW.

Higgins, P. (Editor) (1999). *Handbook of Australian, New Zealand and Antarctic Birds. Volume 4. Parrots to dollarbird.* Oxford University Press, Melbourne.

Higgins, P.J., Peter, J.M. & Steele, W.K. (Editors) (2001). *Handbook of Australian, New Zealand and Antarctic Birds. Volume 5. Tyrant-flycatchers to chats.* Oxford University Press, Melbourne.

Frith, H.J. (Editor) (1976). *Birds in the Australian high country.* Reed Books, Sydney.

Marchant, S. & Higgins, P. (Editors) (1993). *Handbook of Australian, New Zealand and Antarctic Birds. Volume 2. Raptors to lapwing.* Oxford University Press, Melbourne.

Morcombe, M. (2000). *Field guide to Australian birds.* Steve Parish Publishing, Archerfield, Queensland.

Pizzey, G. & Knight, F. (1997). *Field guide*

to the birds of Australia. Angus & Robertson, Melbourne.

Reader's Digest (1990). *Reader's Digest complete book of Australian birds.* Reader's Digest, Sydney.

Simpson, K. & Day, N. (1984). *Field guide to the birds of Australia. A book of identification.* Penguin Books, Ringwood.

Taylor, I. M. & Day, N. (1993). *Field guide to the birds of the ACT.* National Parks Association of the ACT Inc. Canberra.

Frogs and Reptiles

Barker, J., Grigg, G.C. & Tyler, M.J. (1995). *A field guide to Australian frogs.* Surrey Beatty and Sons, Chipping Norton.

Bennett, R. (1997). *Reptiles and frogs of the Australian Capital Territory.* National Parks Association of the ACT Inc. Canberra.

Cogger, H. (2000). *Reptiles and amphibians of Australia.* Reed Books, Sydney.

Griffiths, K. (1997). *Frogs and reptiles of the Sydney region.* University of New South Wales Press, Sydney.

Hero, J.M., Littlejohn, M. & Marantelli, G. (1991). *Frogwatch field guide to Victorian frogs.* Department of Conservation and Environment, Melbourne.

Jenkins, R. & Bartell, R. (1980). *A field guide to the reptiles of the Australian high country.* Inkata Press, Melbourne.

Tyler, M.J. (1999). *Australian frogs: A natural history.* Reed New Holland, Sydney.

Mammals

Grant, T. (1989). *The platypus. A unique mammal.* University of New South Wales Press, Sydney.

Maxwell, S., Burbidge, A.A. & Morris, K. (1996). *The 1996 Action Plan for Australian marsupials and monotremes.* IUCN/SSC Australian Marsupial and Monotreme Specialist Group. Wildlife Australia Endangered Species Program Project number 500. Wildlife Australia, Canberra.

Menkhorst, P.W. (1995). *Mammals of Victoria. Distribution, ecology and conservation.* Oxford University Press, Melbourne.

Menkhorst, P.W. (2001). *Field guide to the mammals of Australia.* Oxford University Press, Melbourne.

Smith, A.P. & Winter, J. (1997). *A key and field guide to the possums, gliders and koala.* Surrey Beatty and Sons, Chipping Norton.

Strahan, R. (Editor) (1995). *A photographic guide to the mammals of Australia.* Reed New Holland, Sydney.

Strahan, R. (Editor) (1995). *The mammals of Australia. Revised edition.* Reed New Holland, Sydney.

Scientific literature

Anstis, M., Alford, R.A. & Gillespie, G.R. (1998). Breeding biology of *Litoria booroolongensis* Moore and *L. lesueuri* Dumeril and Bibron (Anura: Hylidae). *Transactions of the Royal Society of South Australia*, **122**, 33–43.

Australian and New Zealand Environment and Conservation Council (ANZECC). *A national approach to firewood collection and use in Australia.* Commonwealth of Australia, June 2001.

Barrett, G. (2000). Birds on farms: Ecological management for agricultural sustainability. Supplement to *Wingspan*, **10(4)**. Birds Australia, Hawthorn, Victoria.

Barrett, G.W., Ford, H.A. & Recher, H.F. (1994). Conservation of woodland birds in a fragmented rural landscape. *Pacific Conservation Biology*, **1**, 245–56.

Bennett, A.F., Brown, G., Lumsden, L., Hespe, D., Krasna, S. & Silins, J. (1998). *Fragments for the future. Wildlife in the Victorian Riverina (Northern Plains).* Victorian Department of Natural Resources and Environment, Melbourne.

Bennett, A.F., Kimber, S. & Ryan, P. (2000). *Revegetation and wildlife. A guide to enhancing revegetated habitats for wildlife conservation in rural environments. Bushcare Research Report 2/00.* Bushcare National Research and Development Program Research Report.

Bradstock, R.A., Williams, J.E. & Gill, A.M. (Editors) (2002). *Flammable Australia: fire regimes and the biodiversity of a continent.* Cambridge University Press, Cambridge.

Breckwoldt, R. (1983). *Wildlife in the home paddock: Nature conservation for Australian farmers.* Angus & Robertson, Melbourne.

Campbell, A. (1991). *Planning for sustainable farming: The Potter Farmland Plan story.* Lothian, Melbourne.

Chapman, T. (1999). Fussy Black-Cockatoos. *Nature Australia*, Summer 1999-2000, 48-55.

Clarke, P. (1998). *Your bushland: Tips for managing native bush plants in the New England region.* University of New England, Armidale.

Cooper, C.B., Walters, J.R. & Ford, H. (2002). Effects of remnant size and connectivity on the response of brown treecreepers to habitat fragmentation. *Emu*, **102**, 249–56.

Cremer, K.W. (1995). *Willow identification for river management.* CSIRO, Canberra.

Cutten, J.L. & Hodder, M.W. (2002). *Scattered tree clearance assessment in South Australia. Streamlining guidelines for assessment and rural industry extension.* Department of Water, Land and Biodiversity Conservation, South Australia.

Department of Natural Resources and Environment (1999). *Wildlife in Box-Ironbark Forests. Linking research and biodiversity management. Information kit.* Department of Natural Resources and Environment, Melbourne. www.nre.vic.gov.au/notes/

Eddy, D. (2002). *Managing native grass-land. A guide to management for conservation, production and landscape protection.* WWF Australia, Sydney.

Er, K. (1997). Effects of eucalypt dieback on bird species diversity in remnants of native woodland. *Corella,* **21**, 69–76.

Er, K. & Tidemann, C.R. (1996). Importance of Yellow Box-Blakely's Red Gum woodland remnants in maintaining bird species diversity: inferences from seasonal data. *Corella,* **20**, 117-25.

Fischer, J. & Lindenmayer, D.B. (2002a). The conservation value of paddock trees for birds in a variegated landscape in southern New South Wales. I. Species composition and site occupancy patterns. *Biodiversity and Conservation,* **11**, 807–32.

Fischer, J. & Lindenmayer, D.B. (2002b). The conservation value of paddock trees for birds in a variegated landscape in southern New South Wales. II. Paddock trees as stepping stones. *Biodiversity and Conservation,* **11**, 832–49.

Ford, H.A. (1979). Birds. pp. 103-114. In *Natural history of Kangaroo Island.* M.J. Tyler, C.R. Twidale & J.K. Ling (Editors). Royal Society of South Australia, Adelaide.

Ford, H.A., Barrett, G.W., Saunders, D.A. & Recher, H.F. (2001). Why have birds in the woodlands of southern Australia declined? *Biological Conservation,* **97**, 71–88.

Freudenberger, D. (1999). *Guidelines for enhancing grassy woodlands for the Vegetation Investment Project.* CSIRO and Greening Australia, ACT, and SE NSW Inc.

Freudenberger, D. (2001). *Bush for the birds: Biodiversity enhancement guidelines for the Saltshaker Project, Boorowa, NSW.* CSIRO and Greening Australia, ACT, and SE NSW Inc.

Frith, H.J. (Editor) (1976). *Birds in the Australian high country.* Reed Books, Sydney.

Gibbons, P. & Boak, M. (2002). The value of paddock trees for regional conservation in an agricultural landscape. *Ecological Management and Restoration* (in press).

Gibbons, P. & Lindenmayer, D.B. (2002). *Tree hollows and wildlife conservation in Australia.* CSIRO Publishing, Melbourne.

Gillespie, G.R. & Hunter, D. (1999). The Booroolong Frog *Litoria booroolongensis* Moore (Anura: Hylidae): an addition to the frog fauna of Victoria. *The Victorian Naturalist,* **116**, 112–14.

Goldney, D. & Wakefield, S. (1997). *Save the bush toolkit.* Charles Sturt University, Bathurst.

Greening Australia. (2001). *Bringing birds back. A glovebox guide for bird identification and habitat restoration in ACT and SE NSW.* Greening Australia, ACT and SE NSW.

Hamer, A.J., Lane, S.J. & Mahony, M.J. (2002). The role of introduced mosquitofish (*Gambusia holbrooki*) in excluding the native green and gold bell frog (*Litoria aurea*) from original habitats in south-eastern Australia. *Oecologia,* **132**, 445–52.

Hazell, D., Cunningham, R.B., Lindenmayer, D.B. & Osborne, W. (2001). Use of farm dams as frog habitat in an Australian agricultural landscape: factors affecting species richness and distribution. *Biological Conservation*, **102**, 155–69.

Higgins, P. (Editor) (1999). *Handbook of Australian, New Zealand and Antarctic Birds. Volume 4. Parrots to dollarbird.* Oxford University Press, Melbourne.

Higgins, P.J., Peter, J.M. & Steele, W.K. (Editors) (2001). *Handbook of Australian, New Zealand and Antarctic Birds. Volume 5. Tyrant-flycatchers to chats.* Oxford University Press, Melbourne.

Hobbs, R.J. & Yates, C.J. (2000). *Temperate eucalypt woodlands in Australia.* Surrey Beatty and Sons, Chipping Norton.

Hussey, P. & Wallace, K. (1993). *Managing your bushland.* Department of Conservation and Land Management, Perth.

Jansen, A. & Robertson, A.I. (2001). Relationships between livestock management and the ecological condition of riparian habitats along an Australian floodplain river. *Journal of Applied Ecology*, **38**, 63–75.

Jenkins, S. (1998). *Native vegetation on farms survey 1996.* Land and Water Research and Development Corporation, Canberra. Research Report 3/98.

Keogh, J.S. (1999). Evolutionary implications of hemipenal morphology in the terrestrial Australian elapid snakes. *Zoological Journal of the Linnean Society*, **125**, 239–78.

Keogh, J.S. (2000). Snake penises. *Nature Australia*, Winter 2000, 42–9.

Kimber, S., Bennett, A.F. & Ryan, P.A. (1999). *Revegetation and wildlife. What do we know about revegetation and wildlife conservation in Australia?* Report to Environment Australia, Canberra. December 1999.

Lambert, J. & Elix, J. (undated). *Grassy white box woodlands. Information kit.* Community Solutions, Sydney.

Laven, N.H. & Mac Nally, R. (1997). Association of birds with fallen timber in Box-Ironbark forest of central Victoria. *Corella*, **22**, 55–60.

Lee, A.K. & Martin, R.W. (1988). *The koala: A natural history.* University of New South Wales Press, Sydney.

Lindenmayer, D.B., Cunningham, R.B., Tribolet, C.R., Donnelly, C.F. & MacGregor, C. (2001). The Nanangroe Landscape Experiment— baseline data for mammals, reptiles and nocturnal birds. *Biological Conservation,* **101**, 157–69.

Lindenmayer, D.B., Claridge, A.W., Gilmore, A.M., Michael, D. & Lindenmayer, B.D. (2002). The ecological role of logs in Australian forest and the potential impacts of harvesting intensification on log-using biota. *Pacific Conservation Biology*, **8**, 121–140.

Lumsden, L., Bennett, A., Silins, J. & Krasna, S. (1994). *Fauna in a remnant vegetation-farmland mosaic: movements, roosts and foraging ecology of bats.* A report to the Australian Nature Conservation 'Save the Bush' Program. Department of Conservation and Natural Resources, Melbourne.

McIntyre, S., McIvor, J.G. & Heard, K.M. (Editors). (2002). *Managing and conserving grassy woodlands.* CSIRO Publishing, Melbourne.

Mac Nally, R. & McGoldrick, J. (1997). Mass flowering and landscape dynamics of bird communities in some eucalypt forests of central Victoria, Australia. *Journal of Avian Biology*, **28**, 171–83.

Major, R.E., Christie, F.J. & Gowing, G. (2001). Influence of remnant and landscape attributes on Australian woodland bird communities. *Biological Conservation*, **102**, 47–66.

Marchant, S. & Higgins, P. (Editors) (1993). *Handbook of Australian, New Zealand and Antarctic Birds. Volume 2. Raptors to lapwing.* Oxford University Press, Melbourne.

Michael, D.R. (2001). Vertebrate fauna in a semi-arid grassland at Terrick Terrick National Park, Victoria: distributions, habitat preferences and use of experimental refuges. B AppSc. (Hons) thesis. Charles Sturt University, Albury.

Minko, G. & Fagg, P.C. (1989). Control of some mistletoe species on eucalypts by trunk injection with herbicides. *Australian Forestry*, **52**, 94–102.

Page, M.J. & Beeton, R.J. (2000). Is the removal of domestic stock sufficient to restore semi-arid conservation areas? *Pacific Conservation Biology*, **6**, 245–53.

Paton, D. (1991). Loss of wildlife to domestic cats. In *The impacts of cats on native wildlife*. C. Potter, (Editor). The Australian National Parks and Wildlife Service. pp. 64–9.

Platt, S. (2002). *How to plan wildlife landscapes.* Victorian Department of Natural Resources and Environment, Melbourne.

Primary Industries Standing Committee (2002). *Spray Drift Management: Principles, Strategies and Supporting Information.* PISC (SCARM) Report 82. CSIRO Publishing, Melbourne.

Redpath, P. (1999). Unpublished Discussion Paper No. 1. Native Vegetation Branch: Benefits of retained isolated paddock trees and clumps of trees. NSW Department of Land and Water Conservation.

Reid, J.R. (1999). *Threatened and declining birds in the New South Wales Sheep-Wheat belt. I. Diagnosis, characteristics and management.* Consulting Report to NSW National Parks and Wildlife Service, Canberra.

Robinson, D. (1992). Habitat use and foraging behaviour of the Scarlet Robin and the Flame Robin at a site of breeding season sympatry. *Wildlife Research*, **19**, 377–95.

Rutherford, I.D., Jerie, K. & Marsh, N. (2000). *A rehabilitation manual for Australian streams.* Land and Water Research and Development Corporation (Canberra) and Cooperative Research Centre for Catchment Hydrology.

Seddon, J., Briggs, S. & Doyle, S. (2001). *Birds in woodland of the central wheat/sheep belt of New South Wales.* NHT Report. NSW National Parks and Wildlife Service, Canberra. February 2001.

Soderquist, T.R. (1993a). Maternal strategies of *Phascogale tapoatafa* (Marsupialia: Dasyuridae). I. Breeding seasonality and maternal investment. *Australian Journal of Zoology,* **41**, 549–66.

Soderquist, T.R. (1993b). Maternal strategies of *Phascogale tapoatafa* (Marsupialia, Dasyuridae). II. Juvenile thermoregulation and maternal attendance. *Australian Journal of Zoology,* **41**, 567–76.

Soderquist, T.R. & Mac Nally, R. (2000). The conservation value of mesic gullies in dry forest landscapes: mammal populations in the box-ironbark ecosystem of southern Australia. *Biological Conservation,* **93**, 281–91.

Spooner, P., Lunt, I. & Robinson, W. (2002). Is fencing enough? The short-term effects of stock exclusion in remnant grassy woodlands in southern NSW. *Ecological Management and Restoration,* **3**, 117–26.

Stirzaker, R., Vertessy, R. & Sarre, A. (Editors) (2002). *Trees, water and salt. An Australian guide to using trees for healthy catchment and productive farms.* Joint Venture Agroforestry Program, Canberra.

Thompson, L., Jansen, A. & Robertson, A. (2002). *The responses of birds to restoration of riparian habitat on private properties.* Johnstone Centre Report No. 163. Charles Sturt University, Wagga Wagga.

Van der Ree, R. (1999). Barbed wire fencing as a hazard for wildlife. *The Victorian Naturalist,* **116**, 210–17.

Watson, D.M. (2001). Mistletoe—A keystone resource in forests and woodlands worldwide. *Annual Review of Ecology and Systematics,* **32**, 219–49.

Watson, D.M. (2002). Effects of mistletoe on diversity: a case study from southern New South Wales. *Emu,* **102**, 275–81.

Walters, J.R., Ford, H.A. & Cooper, C.B. (1999). The ecological basis of sensitivity of brown treecreepers to habitat fragmentation: A preliminary assessment. *Biological Conservation,* **90**, 13–20.

Whitaker, P.B. & Shine, R. (1999). Responses of free-ranging brown snakes (*Pseudonaja textilis* Elapidae) to encounters with humans. *Wildlife Research,* **26**, 689–704.

Williams, G.A. & Serena, M. (1999). *Living with platypus. A practical guide to the conservation of a very special Australian.* Australian Platypus Conservancy, Whittlesea, Victoria.

Williams, J.E. (2000). *Managing the bush: recent research findings from the EA/LWRRDC National Remnant Vegetation Program.* Land and Water Resources Research and Development Corporation. Research Report 4/00, Canberra.

Wilson, G., Dexter, N., O'Brien, P. & Bomford, M. (1992). *Pest animals in Australia. A survey of introduced wild mammals.* Bureau of Rural Resources, Canberra.

Woinarski, J.C., Recher, H.F. & Majer, J.D. (1997). Vertebrates of eucalypt formations. pp. 303–41. In *Eucalypt ecology. Individuals to ecosystems.* J. Williams & J. Woinarski (Editors). Cambridge University Press, Melbourne.

Index

agile antechinus (*Antechinus agilis*)   70
antechinuses   22, 23, 70–71
apostlebird (*Struthidea cinerea*)   28
azure kingfisher (*Alcedo pusilla*)   56
baiting programs   41–42
banjo frog (*Limnodynastes dumerilii*)   101
bark strips   13–14
basking sites   23, 24, 28
Baw Baw frog (*Philoria frosti*)   93
beach stone-curlew (*Esacus neglectus*) 76
Bibron's toadlet (*Pseudophryne bibronii*)   93, 98–99
black wallaby (*Wallabia bicolor*)   19–20
black wattle (*Acacia mearnsii*)   18
blue gum (*Eucalyptus globulus*)   49
Booroolong frog (*Litoria booroolongensis*)   28, 32, 102–103
branches (fallen)   22–24
brigalow (*Acacia harpopylla*)   54
broad-headed snake (*Hoplocephalus bungaroides*)   25, 60
brown antechinus (*Antechinus stuartii*)   70
brown snake (*Pseudonaja textilis*)   24, 80, 81
brown treecreeper (*Climacteris picumnus*)   14, 23, 27, 74–75
brush-tailed phascogale (*Phascogale tapoatafa*)   12, 41, 45, 50–51
burning   35, 37–38
bush stone-curlew (*Burhinus grallarius*)   2, 23, 26, 42, 43, 44, 76–77
bushrock   25, 26, 34, 35, 43
cane toad* (*Bufo marinus*)   101
carpet python (*Morelia spilota*)   2, 43, 60–61
cat* (domestic or introduced) (*Felis catus*)   41, 43, 64
chemical use   33, 38–39
cinnamon fungus* (*Phytopthora cinnamomi*)   20
clamorous reed-warbler (*Acrocephalus stentoreus*)   29
common bronzewing (*Phaps chalcoptera*) 18
common brushtail possum (*Trichosurus vulpecula*)   12, 54, 64
common eastern froglet (*Crinia signifera*)   92–93
common ringtail possum (*Pseudocheirus peregrinus*)   13, 14, 18, 19, 30, 42, 64–65
common starling* (*Sturnus vulgaris*)   52
creek disturbance   31–32
creeks   28–33, 37
crested shrike–tit (*Falcunculus frontatus*)   13

* introduced species with populations established in Australia
# overseas species but no populations established in Australia

Cunningham's skink (*Egernia cunninghami*)   25, 86–87
cypress pine (*Callitris spp.*)   54
dams   29, 30, 32, 33
dead trees   10, 11, 16, 35
dead wood   14
diamond firetail (*Stagonopleura guttata*)   26, 43, 78–79
diamond python (*Morelia spilota spilota*)   25, 60–61
dieback   2, 12, 20, 21
dollarbird (*Eurystomus orientalis*)   10
dreys   19, 65
dunnart (*Sminthopsis spp.*)   27, 70
dusky toadlet (*Uperoleia fusca*)   100
earthworms   24
eastern rosella (*Platycercus eximus*)   10
eastern sign-bearing frog (*Crinia parinsignifera*)   92
eastern smooth frog (*Geocrinia victoriana*)   93
eastern spinebill (*Acanthorhynchus tenuirostris*)   18
eastern spiny-tailed gecko (*Diplodactylus intermedius*)   84
eastern yellow robin (*Eopsaltria australis*)   18
echidna (*Tachyglossus aculeatus*)   22, 23, 72–73
emu (*Dromaius novaehollandiae*)   18
european rabbit* (*Oryctolagus cuniculus*)   2, 21, 61
farm dams   29, 30, 32, 33
farm forestry   17
farm management,   8–9, 34–43
    for creeks, wetlands and dams   30–33, 37
    for logs, surface rocks and ground cover   26–27
    for trees   16–17
    for understorey trees and shrubs   21
fencing   16–17, 32, 35, 37
feral animals   33, 34, 41–42, 43
fire   11, 17, 21, 26, 33, 34, 35
firewood   16, 34, 35, 43
flame robin (*Petroica phoenicea*)   68
flowers   12
food sources   12–14
forest red gum (*Eucalyptus tereticornis*)   49
frogs   6, 22, 23, 29, 31, 32–33, 62–63, 88–89, 92–103
fruits   12, 18
funding and assistance   1, 39–40
fungi (native truffles)   20
galah (*Cacatua roseicapilla*)   30, 54
gang-gang cockatoo (*Callocephalon fimbriatum*)   14
geckos   13, 22, 27, 84–85
geebung (*Persoonia spp.*)   18
glossy black-cockatoo (*Calyptorhynchus lathamii*)   6, 12, 14, 17, 54–55
golden wattle (*Acacia pycnantha*)   17, 52
golden whistler (*Pachycephala pectoralis*)   66

grasslands   25–26, 27
grazing pressure   26, 31, 35
greater glider *(Petauroides volans)*   17
green and golden bell frog *(Litoria aurea)*   44, 88–89, 95
grey shrike-thrush *(Colluricincla harmonica)*   16, 66
ground cover   22–27, 35
habitat restoration   6, 40–41
habitats,   1–9
    creeks, wetlands and dams   28–33
    and farm management   8–9, 34–43
    logs, surface rocks and ground cover   22–27
    trees   10–17
    understorey trees and shrubs   18–21
heath (Rosenberg's) monitor *(Varanus rosenbergi)*   58
hollows   10–11, 16, 35, 45
honey bee* *(Apis mellifera)*   54
honeyeaters   2, 17, 18, 20, 41
house mouse* *(Mus musculus)*   2
hunting and trapping   43
integrated farm management   34–43
introduced predators   33, 34, 41–42, 43
koala *(Phascolarctos cinereus)*   12, 17, 38, 48–49
Komodo dragon# *(Varanus komodoensis)*   59
kunzea *(Kunzea spp.)*   64
lace monitor (or goanna) *(Varanus varius)*   2, 42, 58–59
leaden flycatcher   14
leaf-litter   13, 23
leaves   12
lerps   12
Lesueur's frog *(Litoria lesueuri)*   102
little lorikeet *(Glossopsitta pusilla)*   52
livestock   17, 31, 32–33, 37
logs   22–24, 26–27
long-thumbed frog *(Limnodynastes fletcheri)*   94
magpie *(Gymnorhina tibicen)*   2, 69
magpie lark *(Grallina cyanoleuca)*   28
manna gum *(Eucalyptus viminalis ssp. viminalis)*   12, 13
marbled gecko *(Christinus marmoratus)*   84–85
mistletoe   11, 14, 15
mistletoe bird *(Dicaeum hirundinnaceum)*   14
mosquito control   33
mosquito fish* *(Gambusia holbrookii)*   33
musk lorikeet *(Glossopsitta concinna)*   52
native grasslands   25–26, 27
native truffles   20
nest boxes   12
nesting places   18–19
noisy friarbird *(Philemon corniculatus)*   13, 14

noisy minor (*Manorina melancephala*)   20, 21
olive legless lizard (*Delma inornata*)   26, 80–81
paddock trees   9, 14, 15, 17
painted honeyeater (*Grantiella picta*)   14
paperbark (*Melaleuca spp.*)   46
peat   33
Peron's tree frog (*Litoria peronii*)   41, 43, 62–63
pet-trade   43, 79
platypus (*Ornithorhynchus anatinus*)   2, 28, 90–91
ploughing   26–27, 37
preserving vegetation   35
pythons   61
rainbow bee–eater (*Merops ornatus*)   10, 56
red fox* (*Vulpes vulpes*)   20, 41, 42, 64
red ironbark (Victoria) (*Eucalyptus tricarpa*)   17, 52
red ironbark (Victoria/NSW) (*Eucalyptus sideroxylon*)   17, 52
red-browed firetail (*Neochmia temporalis*)   18, 78
red-browed treecreeper (*Climacteris erythrops*)   74
red-capped robin (*Petroica goodenovii*)   68
red-necked wallaby (*Macropus rufogriseus*)   18
red-tailed black cockatoo (*Calyptorhyncus banksii*)   54
reduction burns   21, 26, 37–38
remnant vegetation   8, 14, 15, 16–17, 21, 35
revegetation   6, 17, 21, 40–41
revegetation programs   17, 27
ribbon gum (*Eucalyptus viminalis*)   13, 49, 52
river red gum (*Eucalyptus camaldulensis*)   49, 84
roads and tracks   43
robins   68–69
rock skink (*Egernia saxatilis intermedia*)   86
rocks   25, 26, 35
rose robin (*Petroica rosea*)   68
rosellas   17, 21
rufous whistler (*Pachycephala rufiventris*)   44, 57, 66–67
sacred kingfisher (*Todramphus sanctus*)   45, 56–57
salinity   30
salmon-striped frog (*Limnodynastes salmini*)   96
sand monitor (*Varanus gouldii*)   58
sap   12, 13, 18
scarlet robin (*Petroica multicolor*)   1, 13, 57, 68–69
seeds   14
she-oak (*Casuarina spp., Allocasuarina spp.*)   6, 14, 17, 21, 54, 55
silvereyes   17
skinks   13, 22, 23, 27, 82–83, 86–87
smooth toadlet (*Uperoleia laevigata*)   100–101
southern bell frog (*Litoria raniformis*)   88, 95
southern rainbow skink (*Carlia tetradactyla*)   82–83

southern toadlet (*Pseudophryne semimarmorata*)   98
spiny-cheeked honeyeater (*Acanthagenys rufogularis*)   14
spotted marsh frog (*Limnodynastes tasmaniensis*)   94–95
spotted pardalote (*Pardalotus punctatus*)   12
squirrel glider (*Petaurus norfolcensis*)   2, 6, 13, 18, 21, 46–47, 50
stock rotation   21
stock watering points   31
striped legless lizard (*Delma impar*)   80
striped marsh frog (*Limnodynastes peronii*)   96–97
sugar glider (*Petaurus breviceps*)   1, 2, 12, 13, 18, 46, 50
sulphur-crested cockatoo (*Cacatua galerita*)   30
surface rocks   25, 26, 35
swamp gum (*Eucalyptus ovata*)   19–20, 49, 52
swamp wallaby (*Wallabia bicolor*)   19, 20, 41
swift parrot (*Lathamus discolor*)   6, 17, 19, 41, 45, 52–53
tree clearing   30–31
tree dtella (*Gehyra variegata*)   84
tree frogs   89
tree hollows   10–11, 16, 35, 45
tree skink (*Egernia striolata*)   86
tree stumps   16, 35
trees,   10–17
    dead   10, 11, 16, 35
    and farm management   16–17
    as food   12–14
    paddock   9, 14, 15, 17
    understorey   18–21
turquoise parrot (*Neophema pulchella*)   16
Tyler's toadlet (*Uperoleia tyleri*)   100
Tyler's tree frog (*Litoria tyleri*)   62
understorey trees and shrubs   18–21
wattles   18, 19, 21
wedge-tailed eagle (*Aquila audax*)   42
wetlands   28–33, 38
whistling tree frog (*Litoria verreauxii*)   89
white box (*Eucalyptus albens*)   1, 52
white-throated treecreeper (*Cormobates leucophaea*)   74
white-winged chough (*Corcorax melanorhamphos*)   28
whole-farm plan   34
wild dogs   41, 42
willow* (*Salix spp.*)   32
woodlands   7, 26, 38
woodswallow (*Artamus spp.*)   10, 14
yellow box (*Eucalyptus melliodora*)   1, 84
yellow-footed antechinus (*Antechinus flavipes*)   23, 70–71
yellow-rumped thornbill (*Acanthiza chrysorrhea*)   18
yellow-tailed black cockatoo (*Calyptorhyncus funereus*)   54

Reader feedback

The authors of *Wildlife on Farms* welcome your comments on this book. They would like to hear about things that they missed, things that could be improved, or anything that you found particularly useful. Your feedback will mean that future editions of this book can be more valuable for people on the land who are keen to conserve native wildlife.

Please send your comments to:
David Lindenmayer
Centre for Resource & Environmental Studies,
The Australian National University
Canberra ACT 0200

email: davidl@cres.anu.edu.au